ABORTION & LIFE

BY JENNIFER BAUMGARDNER

PHOTOGRAPHS BY TARA TODRAS-WHITEHILL

AKASHIC BOOKS
NEW YORK

Several passages in Chapter 3 and Chapter 6 originally appeared in an earlier form on AlterNet and Nerve, respectively.

Published by Akashic Books
©2008 Jennifer Baumgardner
Photographs ©2008 Tara Todras-Whitehill

ISBN-13: 978-1-933354-59-0
Library of Congress Control Number: 2008925930
All rights reserved

First printing

Akashic Books
PO Box 1456
New York, NY 10009

There is no agony like bearing an untold story inside you.
—Zora Neale Hurston

*The defensiveness that the pro-choice movement has is well-earned.
We've been shot at, picketed, fought every step. But I'm very glad
that the conversation is changing.*
—Loretta Ross

For Barbara Seaman (9/11/35–2/27/08), who really listened

Acknowledgments from Jennifer

This book couldn't have come together without the help of the following people: Amy Ray, Merle Hoffman and the Diana Foundation, Gloria Browning, Karen Burgum and the F-M Area Foundation Women's Fund, and Roberta Schneiderman—all are incredibly generous women who underwrote the research of this book. My friend Gillian Aldrich directed the documentary that was the cornerstone of bringing the "I Had an Abortion" project into being; many of Gillian's interviews are threaded through this book. Rebecca Hyman kindly allowed me to reprint her article about the abortion T-shirts. Conversations on the History in Action listserv provided inspiration, personal stories, and clarity. Merle Hoffman, Constance DeCherney, Soraya Field Fiorio, and Dea Goblirsch read drafts of the text, and Rebecca Davis helped write the resource guide. Intrepid photographer Tara Todras-Whitehill suggested that we use her stunning portraits as the basis for a book; Akashic Books publisher Johnny Temple (a man with integrity to spare) had instant and enduring faith in the project. My deep gratitude goes out to all of the above and to the many women and men who agreed to share their stories—in particular Amy Richards, whose insights continue to evolve my thinking on many issues. Finally, it goes almost without saying that my open-minded family—Skuli, Mom and Dad, and Andrea and Jessica—enable my work on a daily basis. I thank all of the above for their good humor, brains, and honesty.

Tara thanks

My parents for their constant support, even when they weren't sure what I was doing, and especially my mother for being my first subject on this project. My wonderful friends and family—for their encouragement, energy, and faith in my work, without whom I would have given up long, long ago. Patrick McMullen and company, for donating their studio space and lights for these portraits. Modernage, for making such beautiful huge prints of the women. Ken Regan, for being a great photographer, friend, and mentor to whom I will always be grateful. All the people who donated to the creation of the prints so that people could see the women life-sized and eye-to-eye. Jennifer Baumgardner, for seeing the potential of this project and incorporating it into her own without hesitation; additionally, seeing Jennifer's energy and passion about women's issues was instrumental in helping me focus on what was important in my life at a time when I was really searching for direction. And finally, the women who allowed me to photograph them: I can't thank them enough for letting me into their lives and for being such strong role models—they are an inspiration to me and I hope to everyone who sees their pictures.

TABLE OF CONTENTS

INTRODUCTION

I don't remember when I first heard the word *abortion*. What I do recall is this: By age four I knew, generally, how babies were made because my mother became pregnant with my sister Jessica and insisted on explaining to us, in the most clinical and explicit terms possible, about vaginas, sperm, eggs, and intercourse. My parents weren't hippies—far from it, in fact, having been raised in small-town North Dakota during the 1950s. I too was raised in North Dakota, but I was a child of the 1970s and my youth was colored by the cultural movements of the time, including feminism.

The second wave of feminism ushered in consciousness and discussion about birth and bodies, as well as a woman's right to control both of these things herself. My mother recalls showing my Grandma Gladys the photos of childbirth in *Our Bodies, Ourselves* and Grandma—who had given birth to eight children, three when she was still a teenager—saying that she had never glimpsed a baby's head crowning out of a vagina. She was fascinated. We had *Ms.* magazine in the house, with its frequent headlines about reproductive freedom, and I think I absorbed what ending an unwanted pregnancy was before anyone ever talked to me about it.

The first real conversation I had about abortion occurred when I was ten and my family was visiting friends in Iowa City. The mother in that family, Laurel Bar, was a strong feminist, intense and intimidating to me at that age. Laurel had two identical pins the size of half dollars on her kitchen bulletin board, both depicting the pro-choice symbol of that generation—a wire hanger with a red bar struck through it. I was intrigued and asked if I could have one. She held a pin out and looked me right in the eye. "I'll give this to you," she said sternly, "but only if you wear it and understand what it means." Her intensity made me momentarily nervous, but at the same time, I was flattered that she was taking me seriously. I took the button from her, and I took its message to heart. The point of that button was, of course, the assertion that a woman should never be forced to thrust a hanger through her cervix and into her uterus because she is pregnant and has no access to a legal abortion.

For Laurel's generation, for Laurel herself, this hanger meant something literal. Laurel was the sole confidante (with the exception of the girl's mother) to a friend who'd had an illegal abortion in 1964. The girl's mother, who insisted that the father could never find out, had found the abortionist and taken her terrified daughter to an actual back alley to meet her fate. After the abortion, the girl bled copiously. Six years later, Laurel flew with another pregnant friend to New York City, this time for a legal abortion. "The difference was staggering," Laurel now recalls. "The second friend just walked out of the clinic, came back to the hotel, and was completely fine. No secrets; no hemorrhaging."

For my generation in the United States, though, the hanger doesn't evoke memories of barriers that women faced. The image is abstract, not quite relevant—a marker of another time and, despite claims to the contrary, not likely to be part of our future, even if *Roe v. Wade,* the 1973 Supreme Court decision that made abortion legal in all fifty states, were to be overturned.

A current symbol of reproductive freedom—what would that be? A gun with a strike through it to represent the clinic violence that marked the 1980s to mid-'90s, killing three doctors and four other clinic workers? The fleshy pink faces of Senator Jesse Helms and Representative Henry Hyde, both of whom signed into law restrictions that mean poor women have very limited access to early abortion and birth control information? Angels' wings, to indicate the thousands of women who have abortions and yet believe that a fetus has a soul and is watching over them? Or an open mouth, to illustrate the growing movement of women who are speaking out about their abortion experiences, from the after-abortion counseling groups like Backline and Exhale to the zine *Our Truths/Nuestras Verdades* to the films *Silent Choices* and *The Abortion Diaries?* These are some of the images that have animated the last few decades and that speak to the experience of my peers—younger women and men raised in the wake of legal abortion.

After years of thinking and writing about abortion, I have learned many things that bolster my belief that supporting abortion rights (without restrictions) is the most ethical position one can take. I have seen ample evidence that abortion is the result, not the cause, of social problems. Dilemmas such as inadequate access to health care, female poverty, and sexual violence remain pernicious, and there is no doubt that if we addressed those issues, we'd reduce the need for abortion. Seventeen percent of those who terminate unplanned pregnancies are teenagers, many of whom have shrinking access to sex education or birth control since most states accept federal money that mandates abstinence-only education. Meanwhile, women on Medicaid often receive less effective generic forms of the birth control pill that contain only eighty percent of the hormones in brand-name pills. When I hosted poor women who had traveled to New York for abortions, every single one said she got pregnant while on the pill, leading me to believe that generic birth control is a problem that must be addressed.

For those people horrified about abortion—and I am more sympathetic to this perspective than I once was—it is crucial to confront social injustices that precede the embryo, fetus, or baby; and to accept that it might not be possible to ever truly abolish abortion. In fact, countries in which abortion is legal and those in which it is a crime have similar abortion rates, according to a 2007 report by the Guttmacher Institute (generally considered to be the best, most accurate source for reproductive health research) and the World Health Organization; and the abortion rate is dropping more quickly in countries that provide above-ground procedures. But as I explore later in this book, it may nonetheless be possible to be authentically, actively, radically pro-life; learning how to do so *ethically* is the real challenge for people who believe the fetus has a soul.

While I'm absolutely opposed to compulsory pregnancy, I have also evolved my position over the years. I began my pro-choice activism as a gung-ho young feminist who bought into received wisdom and bumper sticker slogans (*Get Your Laws Off My Body!*) more than I trusted my own ability to understand the issue. I had an instinct that abortion rights were intrinsically tied to women's human rights, but I mainly absorbed what others—women I respected—had to say about the issue and its complexities. Since then, I've visited abortion clinics around the country and observed what happens to the remains of eight-week, twelve-week, and fourteen-week aborted fetuses. I have hosted half a dozen women in my tiny apartment, sad ladies who traveled long distances to get twenty-four-week abortions that take three days to accomplish. Since 1995, I have helped raise thousands of dollars to pay for low-income women's abortions, coproduced a documentary of women's abortion stories, sat on the board of an abortion fund, and I've written on the subject for at least ten magazines, from the *Nation* to *Glamour* to *Jane*.

I haven't had an abortion to date, but I did become accidentally pregnant in 2004. That unplanned event resulted in my son Skuli and deepened my gratitude for how things have changed because of the feminist movement of the '60s and '70s. Would I have been so encouraged to have a child out of wedlock without that movement? Would I have thrived if I didn't have access to a good job and the sense that a woman shouldn't be dependent on a man any more than a fish be dependent on a bicycle? My pregnancy actually increased my interest in abortion. I embarked on a campaign called the "I Had an Abortion" project in late 2003, and by the time the film of the same name was nearly complete in late 2004, my appreciation for the profundity of the issue was growing, like my body, every day.

The more I began to talk to people about their abortion experiences, the more questions I had. Really basic queries that I had simply never asked myself, such as: *How do women experience abortion? How do men experience it?*

That led to: *Why aren't there more after-abortion resources? Why aren't more women allowed to invite their partners into the procedure room (or anywhere besides the waiting room) if it has been established that they want the support?* And: *If you admit you are sad about your abortion, does that mean abortion is wrong? Can you be a feminist and pro-life? What happens to birth mothers dealing with adoption? If you aren't at all sad about getting rid of your pregnancy, can you admit that publicly without being called a monster?*

After years of interviewing women about their abortion experiences, I still see myself in the ten-year-old girl who solemnly accepted a no-more-coat-hangers pin to wear. I honor the women who lived through that time. Even so, my role as an advocate for abortion rights has moved from winning support for pro-choice legislation to examining how this generation's experience of abortion is shifting. I want to thereby shed light on the ethics and laws that dictate women's human rights, and I believe our personal stories will tell us where the political movement needs to go.

Can storytelling—mere talking—truly protect our rights? Our personal stories give the movement its authenticity. Our personal stories actually strengthen our political position. And fortunately I'm not alone in this belief. During the fall of 2007, Dr. Susan Wicklund called for more openness about the stories behind abortion in her book *This Common Secret: My Journey as an Abortion Provider*. Former Planned Parenthood President Gloria Feldt looked to personal experiences for her 2003 book *Behind Every Choice Is a Story*. Likewise, the independent providers who make up the Abortion Conversation Project have been creating connective tissue between the issue and the women they serve for more than a decade. (A recent initiative, called "Mom, Dad, I'm Pregnant," generates resources to help girls communicate with their parents about their pregnancy, as it is a time when most girls really need the support of their parents or other trusted adults.) In 2004, the Feminist Women's Health Center, based in Washington State, produced a report entitled, "Listening to the Women We Serve: Young Women's Attitudes about Abortion and Choice." The report found that most of the women coming to clinics for abortions rarely

thought about the subject, believed most people were opposed to the procedure, didn't know that one-third of women in the U.S. would have at least one
abortion in their lives, and nearly half did not vote *nor identify* as pro-choice.
However, explains Portland-based activist Grayson Dempsey in a speech in
which she discussed the report, "When put in focus groups with other women
where they could talk openly about their experiences," women suddenly connected to the issue. Those same "apathetic" women became outraged at the
restrictions on abortion that were being introduced and passed at the state and
federal levels. Ultimately, Dempsey noted, some of these women got mobilized
and became activists and pro-choice voters. It began with a personal conversation, a chance to talk with other women about what had happened to them.
Speaking out about their own stories led to a political awakening and was a
catalyst for becoming activists.

People often question whether or not this is a good time to speak openly
and truthfully about the more controversial issues surrounding abortion.
Given the many enemies this legal procedure has, aren't we just handing
antiabortion foes fodder if we talk about the fact that some women feel like
the clinic was a factory experience, or if we encourage women to discuss their
ambivalent feelings about the fetus? Why examine the gory aspects of later-
term procedures?

There are many reasons, to my mind, that space for honesty is crucial right
now. The first is to identify places where the actual provision of terminations—
and abortions are first and foremost an issue of public health—can be im-
proved for the patient. We want a clinic experience that is medically sound
and patient-sensitive. Since abortion is so rarely treated as a medical issue,
though, another critical reason that open conversation should be encouraged is to provide entry points *within the pro-choice movement* for the person
who is ambivalent. "The extreme pro-choice side is clear and confirmed,"
says feminist author Amy Richards, "and the extreme pro-life community
is concrete and resolved too. But those two sides taken together represent
a tiny minority." She is right. The vast majority of Americans don't want

abortion to be recriminalized but are uncomfortable talking about and even facing the realities of the procedure.

Few women who have unplanned pregnancies today have personal experiences of a time when aborting was illegal or when being a single mother meant social doom. The days when a woman or girl had to be willing to pay any sum and endure any danger or humiliation in order to get an abortion are for the most part over, and we are grateful for that. Meanwhile, the generation that has lived with the rights that our mothers' generation fought so hard for has the opportunity to move the abortion issue forward; it has been hopelessly gridlocked for most of my life as a battle between the life of a woman and the life of a fetus. It's not a step back into pre-feminist times to feel differently about the fetus, procedures, and unplanned pregnancy than our mothers' contemporaries did and often still do.

The battle for abortion rights unfolds in a generational way because women who get pregnant today do so in a time where we simply know more about fetuses than other generations did: We see sonograms, experience sophisticated prenatal testing, and read dramatic stories about babies born at twenty-three weeks gestation managing to survive. Science has discovered much about fetal development in the years since 1973. Delicate, lifesaving or spine-repairing surgery can now be performed on a fetus that is only five months old and while in the womb, as has been documented by photos of the Nashville surgeon Dr. Joseph Bruner operating on the twenty-one-week-old fetus Samuel Armas. A preemie born as young as twenty-two weeks (going to full term is thirty-seven to forty weeks of gestation) and weighing just ten ounces can now live if medical care is provided until he or she is around five pounds.

Women who get pregnant today know that it is no longer a social death sentence for being a single mother or having a child out of wedlock; in fact, in 2005, thirty-seven percent of children were born outside of marriage in the U.S., a rate which has been increasing since 1970. Meanwhile, the teen pregnancy rate is decreasing (now at the lowest level in sixty-five years, according to the CDC's National Center for Health Statistics), and the rate of women in their thirties and even forties having children is on the rise, many of them unmarried. As mentioned, I have a child, whom I quite contentedly raise—from separate homes—with his father, Gordon, and we were never married. Abstinence-only education is passing for sexuality education, but most young people have access to online information about sex, diseases, and birth control that was exponentially harder to find even in the '80s, at the height of comprehensive sex ed.

Most significantly, the map of the states where abortion procedures are available has changed irrevocably. If *Roe* were overturned, I would be horrified and sad, but not because it would return us to the bloody, repressive past. In 1967, abortion was illegal in all fifty states; in 1973, before the *Roe* decision, it was legal in just four. If we lost the protection of *Roe* today, there would be a good twenty states in which abortion would still be legal. Those would be the states where it is currently the least difficult to access abortion. In other words, if you are worried about what would happen if *Roe* were overturned, you are already seeing it. The women who would be most affected are the exact ones (young and/or poor women) who already lack access.

Recalibrating our views on abortion can represent real progress, as a woman can now afford to acknowledge that she may be emotionally conflicted about the life growing inside her. She can be openly sad about what ending a pregnancy might mean to her: a break with her religion, a conflict with her sense of self, perhaps even recognition that the relationship she is in can't support this development.

Women and men who are involved with abortions today have complex experiences and stories. More than a few of us young feminists have a growing belief that a fetus is something more than just a blob of tissue. This understanding is buoyed by the incredible view that modern technology gives us of the inside of a womb. Today's abortion rights movement has to come to terms with the truth of graphic antiabortion images, which is that fetuses *have* fingers and toes as early as nine weeks.

And like our second-wave counterparts, women who have abortions to-day are in good company—one in three women will have an abortion by the age of forty-five. And yet these same women often feel very alone in their experiences. There is still mass secrecy surrounding this particular pregnancy event. My hope for this book (and the inspiration for the "I Had an Abortion" project) is to undermine that big shameful *secret*. First, by reviewing the history of abortion and abortion laws; next, by telling women's stories and putting faces, literally, on the issue; and finally, by looking at what the future of reproductive justice might entail. I have also included a resource guide in the back of this volume with just a fraction of the innovative activist groups, films, and books that delve into the issue of abortion rights; and I offer some suggestions about how to strengthen a woman's right to control her body and her life in today's changing political landscape.

Some of what I write might be seen as turning away from the radical history of abortion rights in search of a compromised "middle ground." I would argue, however, that the cornerstones of a new feminist theory of abortion rights will be created by those whom unplanned pregnancy most urgently affects—women born post-*Roe*. Still, as in the past, abortion is a part of life—just as sex and death are. Abortion is not new: The ancient Egyptians had recipes for abortion-inducing medicines, and some female slaves in the antebellum U.S. practiced abortion rather than creating more slaves upon whom their masters could build their fortunes. As these enslaved women demonstrated, abortion is intricately connected to being a parent—the vast majority of women who get abortions will also become mothers or are already mothers. "Women have the power to give life," as health and human rights activist Loretta Ross says (echoed by many women throughout this book), "and we have the power to not give life."

CHAPTER 1

A BRIEF HISTORY OF ABORTION

Despite its enduring controversy, abortion is a very common, if silenced, experience. Each year there are more than a million legal abortions in the U.S. The number has gone down slightly in recent years (from 1.31 million abortions annually in 2000 to 1.21 million five years later), in part due to better use of more effective contraceptives, and possibly linked to the virginity-abstinence movement as well. Lack of access and affordability have also been factors. (Although it's shortsighted, when faced with a slim deadline to raise money and make this decision, some women simply miss the window in which they can have an abortion.) The abortion rate for women below the poverty line is more than four times that of middle-income women. It is estimated that more than thirty-five percent of American women will have an abortion before the age of forty-five, according to the Guttmacher Institute, which notes that the U.S. has a very high abortion rate compared to other industrial nations.

Jewish women have abortions, evangelical Christian women have them, so do Pagans. Catholic women have a slightly higher rate of abortions than Protestant or Jewish women, possibly due to the Vatican ban on contraception. Liberal women like Barbara Ehrenreich and Byllye Avery have abortions, as do conservative women like Dr. Laura Schlessinger, the ultra-judgmental radio talk show host, and Susan Carpenter-McMillan, Paula Jones's mentor and handler during her lawsuit against then-President Bill Clinton. (Carpenter-McMillan has had two.) Even fervent pro-life activists have abortions. Many people who have worked in women's health clinics have seen someone they recognized as a pro-life protester furtively come inside to terminate an unwanted pregnancy.

Abortion in the U.S. is safe. The death rate at all stages is 0.6 per 100,000 abortions. This is said to be as harmless as getting a penicillin injection and nearly ten times as safe as carrying a pregnancy to full term. This high degree of safety is primarily a result of the fact that abortion is legal. Back when abortion was still illegal nationwide, roughly two hundred women died from abortions in 1965 alone. Doctors who practiced pre-*Roe* remember "septic wards" full of women terribly harmed from botched abortions. It's crucial to understand abortion rights in terms of women's most basic ability to live in freedom—or to live at all. Legalizing abortion in the U.S. immediately ended once-common killers of pregnant women like septicemia and bleeding to death from an amateur D&C. It is a "public health advance on a par with the polio vaccine," said the late women's health writer Barbara Seaman, who had an illegal (but "clean") abortion in 1953. Legal abortion is often ranked as one of the true medical milestones of the twentieth century, along with the creation of modern antibiotics and widespread immunization.

The term *reproductive freedom* has only been in use in this country for the past thirty years or so and is currently being reframed as *reproductive justice* (so as to more fully include the experiences of women of color and poor women, who may have never had a "choice"), yet the history of abortion rights in America began much earlier. During the late 1700s, the newly minted republic subscribed to the reproductive mores of England. According to British common law, abortion before "quickening" (prior to the fetus being large enough that a pregnant woman could feel its movements) was legal and performed by a fairly diverse array of practitioners, including midwives and the relatively nascent profession of doctors. After the first sign of a fetal kick, ending a pregnancy was against the law. Soon, however, a movement to outlaw abortion at all stages of gestation was founded by physicians aiming to professionalize their none-too-credible (at the time) line of work.

The first state to impose restrictions on abortion was Connecticut, in 1821. This was not, as one might imagine, due to concern for the woman or even the fetus. Doctors who were beginning to corner the medical market wanted to remove the competition of midwives, practitioners of folk medicine, and herbalists—many of whom were, not coincidentally, women. (The Salem Witch Trials were one tragic effect of the movement to purge women from controlling reproduction—many of the so-called witches killed were herbalists and midwives.) Despite the energy devoted to criminalizing abortion, by the mid-1800s, it was estimated that twenty to twenty-five percent of all pregnancies ended with the procedure, the same percentage that is reported today. When the American Medical Association was founded in 1847, certain types of abortion were illegal in several states. By the turn of the century, the combined forces of Victorian morality and the rising prestige of doctors meant that there was not a single state without an antiabortion statute.

Certain moments in twentieth century history brought waves of pragmatism regarding abortion laws. For instance, during the Great Depression of the 1930s, when there was little money or work for Americans and most families were experiencing some malnutrition, women obtained safe, illegal abortions relatively easily; simultaneously, the prosecution of abortion providers declined. Conversely, other political and cultural tides were beginning to elicit a clampdown on reproductive rights. During the 1950s and early 1960s, for example, while Americans were under the thrall (or fist) of the anti-Communist Red Scare and smarting from the first battles of the sexual revolution, abortion again went underground. This era saw a steep rise in maternal deaths from botched abortions, especially among poor women and women of color.

At a certain point, though, many doctors could no longer ignore the moral obligation they felt to help their female patients receive safe procedures. A small but growing coalition of doctors was galled by the sight of women dying from septicemia in their emergency rooms. Certain progressive clergy joined them in calling for abortion law "reform," meaning that access to terminations would still be tightly controlled by physicians, but it would be much easier to garner a "therapeutic" procedure (an abortion induced for the mental or physical health of the mother). By 1967, a poll of forty thousand physicians conducted by Modern Medicine found that a full eighty-seven percent favored liberalizing the existing abortion laws, including forty-nine percent of Catholic doctors. Meanwhile, men of the cloth such as Reverend Howard Moody of New York's Judson Memorial Church began making abortion referrals. There was even a nationwide Clergy Consultation Service on Abortion composed of rabbis and ministers willing to help women find safe, illegal terminations.

This growing reform coalition converged with a women's movement that was ascendant by 1969. These female activists—freshly radicalized in the antiwar and civil rights movements and accustomed to the convenience of the pill—didn't want mere reform. Reform meant that women would still be subject to convincing individual doctors that a given patient was crazy, or suicidal, or otherwise "deserving" of a termination. Early second-wave feminists, notably Lucinda Cisler of New York City, wanted to repeal *all* antiabortion laws—"abortion on demand, without apology" became their mantra. The fact of abortion being underground was inhumane on many levels. In addition to facing death or infertility due to infection, numerous women who received abortions in the years before *Roe* reported being raped or otherwise molested by their abortionists. (See *Abortion Rap* by Florynce Kennedy and Diane Schulder, which draws from depositions taken from women who had illegal abortions in the years before *Roe*.) Many others have said that they knew of such rapes at the time. One woman spoke about coming out of the anesthesia to find the man who had just performed the procedure standing by her "in bloody undershorts, murmuring depravities." Purely out of choicelessness, many suffered through the degradation and expense of illegal procedures, and once they realized how many others had suffered through similar experiences, they began wondering aloud and angrily why such a necessary and common medical procedure had been denied to them.

Additionally, women who didn't necessarily think of themselves as feminists drew attention to the cause. The most famous was Sherri Finkbine, a young mother and television star, who took thalidomide, a sedative given to pregnant women in the '60s to combat morning sickness, and then found out that it was likely that her child would be born with severe birth defects. At first she was approved to have an abortion in one of the major hospitals in Phoenix by the leading OB/GYN in town. Finkbine, then the host of the popular TV show *Romper Room*, told her story to a reporter because she wanted to warn other women about the dangers of thalidomide to their pregnancies. The resulting media explosion provoked her doctor and the hospital to back out and Finkbine ended up having to travel to Sweden for her procedure. It was outrageous that Finkbine was forced to jump through these hoops for necessary health care, but the resulting publicity helped awaken the American populace to the need for abortion rights.

Feminists began organizing their own underground referral networks for women who needed abortions. Claire Moses, now a professor at the University of Maryland, recalls the anxiety and cloak-and-dagger nature of the time:

I used to keep a carefully maintained list of illegal, but seemingly safe, abortionists in my files. Who knew if or when I, or a friend, would need this? I myself never did have an abortion, but the teenage sister of a very dear friend did, and younger sister called upon older sister, so I was quite involved in the search for names. Everything was sleazy about that search: My friend had to meet first with the abortionist on a dark street corner, and the procedure itself was done at my apartment. Six weeks or so later, the younger sister was either pregnant "again" (which was possible) or, we wondered, was there never an abortion (also possible)? In any case, my friend got the abortionist to agree to (re)do the procedure—this time for an additional price above his regular price, which was agreeing to his fucking my friend right after the abortion was performed on her sister. Anyway, that was in the mid-1960s. After that, we put together a better list of names than we'd had before, which I kept until January 22, 1973, when I happily ripped it up and threw it away.

The most famous informal referral network was in Chicago, Illinois, and was called the Jane Collective, or just "Jane." Jane was unique in that it was launched quite informally by a University of Chicago student named Heather Booth who helped the young sister of a friend find someone who would perform an abortion. There was such demand for abortions that Booth soon found herself overwhelmed with requests. She formed the Jane Collective and then receded from the group to continue with other kinds of activism. When the housewives, students, and activists who formed the collective discovered that the "doctor" they'd been referring women to for years was just a medical technician and not a physician, they decided to take matters into their own hands. Many members learned how to perform abortions themselves, deciding it was worth the legal risk—after all, abortion was a crime whether or not a doctor performed the task. The collective provided between 11,000 and 13,000 procedures at affordable prices before they were closed down in a police bust in 1972. Years later, Jane members revealed how scared they had been performing the abortions and the wide range of responses the women who came to them had. Many were grateful for the compassion and daring of these women (and the low cost), while others had been terrified to go through with this procedure in a random apartment, lying on a shower curtain, with no licensed medical care.

This era of radical feminist activism effectively punctured much of the mystique that had been created around doctors and abortion. The abortion self-help movement joined the women's health movement in suggesting that women themselves were the experts on their own bodies. With books such as *Our Bodies, Ourselves* and activists who taught women how to do "menstrual extractions" (a very early vacuum aspiration performed manually at the time of a missed period), women were refusing to continue taking their lack of reproductive freedom lying down.

On the West Coast, Lorraine Rothman and Carol Downer were the Thelma and Louise of the movement. They made illegal abortion referrals, learned do-it-yourself gynecology, created the very first Feminist Women's Health Center, and were famous for whipping out specula and mirrors to show women how to look at their own vaginas and cervixes. (Due to that last action, Downer was arrested for "practicing medicine without a license.") In 1971, Rothman invented a device that could perform very early menstrual extractions using a Mason jar, aquarium tubing, and a syringe. Soon after, Rothman and Downer led a self-help gynecology class at the Aradia Clinic in Seattle. "We just called [the device] a menstrual extraction kit at the time; it didn't have a name," recalls Downer. While most of their experiences in self-help were met positively, at this clinic they encountered a doctor who was visibly hostile to their demonstration. "She waved her finger in the air like a baton and said, 'How do you clean that *dirty little machine?*'" says Downer. "It cracked us up, so we started calling it the 'dirty little machine' as an in-joke." They shortened the name to DLM, which they pronounced as Del-Em. "We were a bit sassy and arrogant, because we knew how great this thing was," says Downer, who has performed more than 100 menstrual extractions and has seen, by her own admission, thousands of women's cervixes. "We felt irreverent about doctors," she continues, "but even though we felt the name was tongue-in-cheek about the fact that abortion was so hushed up and considered morally 'dirty,' and was, pre-*Roe*, extremely dangerous, the last thing we wanted women to think was that we had dirty equipment, or that we were being cavalier." Thus, they suppressed the name's origins, but rather than abandon it altogether, Rothman declared that Del-Em stood for the "deliberate emptying of the menses."

Margaret Mead once congratulated Rothman for having succeeded in producing the most original and important new product of the twentieth century. (Still, post-*Roe*, the problem with menstrual extraction, as Merle Hoffman explained to me, is that if you are pregnant, there is a fifty percent chance that you will remain pregnant; and if you are not pregnant, you are doing an unnecessary procedure and risk infection.) Menstrual extraction and the Del-Em never became widely popular—in part because abortion became legal in 1973 and women didn't have to resort to home procedures anymore—yet the invention cemented Rothman's historical significance.

On the East Coast, a group called Redstockings began holding speak-outs where they testified about their illegal abortions, a shocking action at the time—and one that attracted media and encouraged other women to act up. Sue Perlgut, a second-wave feminist, says that she was the one who made the initial suggestion that the women confess their own abortions publicly. Rosalyn Baxandall, now a distinguished professor at SUNY College at Old Westbury and then a Redstockings activist, stood up in front of reporters to tell about her illegal abortion. She was terrified about her prudish grandmother reading about it in the news, but her grandmother soon revealed that she had had *thirteen* abortions. Iconic women's rights leader Gloria Steinem, who later signed a statement in *Ms.* magazine coming out about her own illegal abortion, first realized she was a feminist while covering one of these speak-outs. "It was only then," recalls Steinem, "that I realized how little I was alone" in having had an abortion experience.

In 1969, New York feminists interrupted hearings on abortion held by physicians and legislators and demanded to know why women weren't being called on to give "expert" testimony. After all, what did even well-meaning priests, nuns, and male doctors and legislators know about dealing with an unwanted pregnancy? In February of that year, NARAL—the National Association for the Repeal of Abortion Laws (now known as NARAL Pro-Choice America) was cofounded by Larry Lader to organize exclusively around the issue of abortion. By 1970, Planned Parenthood formally voted to support abortion rights, expanding its already broad family planning agenda.

In March 1970, Hawaii became the first state to pass a broad abortion legalization bill, although it went into effect without the signature of the state's Catholic governor. Then, in April 1970, New York State passed the most liberal abortion law in the country (followed that same year by Alaska and Washington): Abortion could be had for *any* reason up through the twenty-fourth week. Those liberal laws and cultural currents set the stage for the Supreme Court case that currently guarantees abortion rights for women throughout the U.S.

Roe v. Wade

By 1970, there were class-action suits pending in several states on behalf of women who wanted abortions. The intention was for the suits to fail on the state level and thereby be brought to the Supreme Court, with the goal of legalizing abortion in general. Emily Jane Goodman, now a New York State Supreme Court Judge, was a young lawyer in 1970 filing amicus briefs that had resulted in New York becoming one of the first states to allow abortion. "I remember the lawyers on the New York abortion case wishing we'd gotten to go to the Supreme Court," says Goodman. "We were *too* successful—the law was changed in this state soon after the case here was filed."

The tide was beginning to turn. That year, Sarah Weddington and Linda Coffee, two lawyers in Austin, Texas, put together a case with a sole plaintiff—a twenty-two-year-old woman with a hard-knock life, two previous children she wasn't able to raise, and an unwanted pregnancy. The young woman, Norma McCorvey, agreed to be "Jane Roe," the pseudonymous plaintiff in *Roe v. Wade.* (Henry Wade was the district attorney in Dallas, Texas.) McCorvey has said that she believed by becoming "Roe," she would be able to get an abortion, not realizing how long the case would take. On January 22, 1973, the U.S. Supreme Court issued a ruling in *Roe v. Wade* finding that the constitutional right to privacy encompasses a woman's right to decide to terminate her own pregnancy. Justice Harry Blackmun wrote the historic decision for seven of the justices; two dissented.

One evening while reading the paper and enjoying an after-work beer with her girlfriend Connie, Norma McCorvey's "eyes wandered to the lower right-hand corner of the page," as she wrote in her 1994 autobiography, *I Am Roe*. "There was a small, matter-of-fact article that said that the United States Supreme Court had legalized abortion all over the United States. That it was now perfectly okay to get an abortion in Texas, or anywhere else." *Roe* had overturned state laws against abortion and, by making it a decision between a *woman* and her doctor (not both people responsible for the pregnancy; and not solely the doctor or psychiatrist, as before), enshrined a woman's right to self-determination more than any decision or law before or since.

McCorvey, then twenty-five and working as a house painter, was very moved by the news: "I knew what it meant to want an abortion," she wrote, "and not be able to have one." While she never had to show up in court and was barely kept in the loop of the various lower court decisions, Norma Mc-Corvey sensed that this was something big. That she was now in the pages of history. And she was—even if Lyndon B. Johnson, the thirty-sixth president of the United States, died that same January 22, 1973, garnering the above-the-fold headlines in all papers of note the next day and obscuring the historic Supreme Court decision. Then, on January 27, a peace deal was struck in Vietnam and *Roe* had missed its news cycle.

Change, however, was felt immediately. Abortion could no longer be outlawed anywhere in the U.S. The women in the Jane Collective who had been busted in Chicago found the charges against them dropped. A companion case to *Roe*, *Doe v. Bolton*, struck down a Georgia law prohibiting abortion except in cases of medical necessity, fetal abnormality, rape, or incest, finding it unconstitutional in the face of *Roe*. Another Georgia law holding that all abortions be performed in accredited hospitals and that three doctors and a committee agree with the woman's decision to abort was also held to violate a woman's constitutional rights, as recognized in *Roe*.

Women celebrated. "I threw a party in an office I had access to. There was a big hardwood floor and we danced most of the night that *Roe* came down," remembers the writer Marge Piercy. "I had worked on getting women illegal abortions for years before that, ever since I had almost died at eighteen of a self-induced abortion. I once cared for a woman hemorrhaging after an abortion while the doctor who had done it claimed [on the phone] he had never heard of her. I packed her with ice and held her. I was terrified she would die." *Roe* meant the kind of hideous, humiliating, and dangerous experiences Piercy described were no longer just "facts of life" if you were a woman.

The right to privacy, upon which the right to abortion is based, is a component of the liberties protected by the Fourteenth Amendment to the Constitution. That amendment reads in part:

No State shall make or enforce any law which shall abridge the privileges or immunities of citizens of the United States; nor shall any State deprive any person of life, liberty, or property, without due process of law; nor deny to any person within its jurisdiction the equal protection of the laws.

The right to privacy was recognized in Supreme Court decisions protecting an individual's bodily integrity as early as the late nineteenth century. It had been applied specifically to the cause of reproductive freedom in 1965. That was the year the Supreme Court ruled on a challenge brought by Estelle Griswold, executive director of the Planned Parenthood League of Connecticut, to overturn the state's ban on the prescription of contraceptives for married people. In *Griswold v. Connecticut*, the Supreme Court held that laws banning the sale of contraceptives were unconstitutional. The court wrote:

The present case . . . concerns a relationship lying within the zone of privacy created by several fundamental constitutional guarantees. And it concerns a law which, in forbidding the use of contraceptives . . . [has] a maximum destructive impact upon that relationship. Such a law cannot stand.

Married couples now had the right to seek birth control in all fifty states. So many pieces of the reproductive rights picture were coming into focus around *Roe*. Since 1970, Title X of the Public Health Service Act meant that poor women had a federal program dedicated to family planning, and by the time *Roe* was decided the national mood appeared poised to ratify the Equal Rights Amendment, ensuring women a secure place in the Constitution. Pro-choice activists thought they had won. Many assumed that they could relax and just devote themselves to providing services. As it turned out, that assumption was naïve.

Antichoice groups, on the other hand, were galvanized by the success of *Roe*. The National Right to Life Committee was founded in 1973, providing coherence for various ad hoc and state-based groups already responding to relaxation of state abortion bans. Under this new national aegis, pro-life activists began organizing politically from the precinct level on up, eventually taking control of the Republican Party's machinery. They attacked at every policy level, chipping away at access, while many pro-choice legislators responded with appeasement rather than either counterattack or creation of an affirmative agenda to expand what *Roe* had accomplished.

Carol Hanisch, an early member of New York Radical Women and scribe of the position paper that launched the phrase "the personal is political" into the public consciousness, recalls her disappointment with *Roe* in this recent e-mail discussion:

> *I was enough involved with the "abortion repeal" movement that I had mixed feelings about Roe. I was glad for the advance but feared that it would mean the end of struggle as women got complacent thinking they had won it all. We hadn't really won "abortion on demand" but only "choice" for those women who fit the criteria of the court, even though it was spun that Roe was a victory for all women—and not only by the mass media, but by the middle-class liberal wing of the WLM [women's liberation movement]. The big liberal abortion groups are still pitching to "save Roe" and "choice" instead of fighting to extend reproductive rights for all women.*

Though flawed according to some activists and legal scholars, *Roe* was and remains a cornerstone feminist decision—one that affirms a woman's right to freedom and the pursuit of happiness. The Supreme Court decision introduced the concept of abortion without apology and full childbearing choice into law. According to *Roe,* a woman didn't have to prove she was deserving (i.e., she was crazy or had been raped) of the choice to abort an unwanted pregnancy in the first trimester. (*Roe* stated that in the second trimester the state had the right to restrict based on situation, and in the third trimester an abortion could only be performed to save the life of the mother.) Still, this liberating concept within the decision—that a woman could decide *herself* whether she would continue with the pregnancy—was part of a huge cultural shift occurring more generally in the 1970s. Not only were women able to control their fertility, they could now participate more fully as decision makers in our society. During this heady and rapidly changing time, women flooded into the workplace in all fields, including those like fire fighting and engineering that were once considered the province of men. *Roe* wasn't fully responsible for women's radical shift in stature, but it facilitated a crucial element of human rights for them: the power to control one's body and thus one's destiny.

In other ways, however, *Roe* and the women's liberation movement were not strong or broad enough (nor had the culture changed enough) to make abortion rights truly accessible to all women. Within a few years of *Roe,* antichoice legislators were finding chinks in *Roe*'s armor and exploiting them. Meanwhile, the most vulnerable women—poor, young, or both—were the first to see that choice still might not apply to them.

A Chill Wind Blows

In 1976, the Hyde Amendment was passed, eliminating federal funding for abortions. The following year, Rosie Jiménez, a twenty-seven-year-old mother of a four-year-old and a recipient of Medicaid, died of the complications from her illegal abortion. Jiménez was just the first known victim of restrictions on legalized abortion and the Hyde Amendment became one of the first major steps backwards after *Roe*.

Senator Jesse Helms (along with other congressional leaders) made sure that no U.S. funds would be spent overseas on abortions, and fought the United Nations on its pro-women and pro–reproductive health care initiatives. Women in the military still have no access to abortion through the military health care system—even if they use their own money and are posted overseas. In 1988, a seventeen-year-old girl by the name of Becky Bell died of a botched illegal procedure; she became the first recorded incident of someone dying because a parental consent law had restricted her from choosing a legal abortion. Bell's parents were devastated—they would have preferred to know about their daughter's abortion, of course, but didn't believe she should have been forced by the state to do so. After her death, they publicly opposed parental consent laws, testifying firsthand that a young woman who doesn't want to tell her parents she's pregnant is not going to do it simply because legislation says she must.

In the years following *Roe*, as the makeup of the Supreme Court changed, the original 7-2 majority slowly eroded. In *Planned Parenthood of Southeastern Pennsylvania v. Casey*, the 1992 Supreme Court reaffirmed women's right to abortion, but at the same time retreated from *Roe* by granting states greater latitude to restrict access. Chief Justice William Rehnquist, one of the two dissenting votes in *Roe*, wrote in *Casey*, "Roe continues to exist, but only in the way a storefront on a Western movie set exists: a mere façade to give the illusion of reality." Justice Harry Blackmun, the hero of *Roe*, remarked after another decision, *Webster v. Reproductive Health Services* (1989), that a "chill wind blows" for the cause of reproductive rights.

In recent years, the rates of both abortion and unplanned pregnancy in the U.S. have been on the decline. In 1987, fifty-seven percent of pregnancies were unplanned, but in 1994, the figure had dropped to forty-nine percent (according to the Guttmacher Institute in 1998, based on figures from the National Surveys of Family Health) and the rate of abortion continued its downward spiral. Data from 2008 show abortions at the lowest rate since 1974. Some of the decline is related to strict demographics: The baby boomers are no longer in their childbearing years. Another factor has to do with better methods of birth control; Guttmacher reported in 2006 that "approximately fourteen percent of the decline in teen pregnancy between 1995 and 2002 was due to teens' delaying sex or having sex less often, while eighty-six percent was due to an increase in contraceptive use." Injectables such as Depo-Provera (a shot given once every three months) are nearly infallible—though they raise concerns about the long-term use of hormones. (Injectables are useful for people with chaotic lives who may not be able to remember to take pills daily, religious women who may need to hide their birth control methods from their partners, and women in abusive relationships who have experienced birth control sabotage.) Many experts attest that, above all, it is the hard work of health care providers to make sure that people have the information and access to birth control that accounts for the decline in abortions.

Even so, despite the legality and technical availability of abortion, several factors continue to diminish women's access to this constitutionally protected right. These factors can be generalized into four areas:

Restrictions

The 1992 *Casey* decision trimmed back the protections provided by *Roe*, holding that state-imposed restrictions are permissible as long as they do not constitute an "undue burden" to the woman. Common restrictions that courts have thus far found not to be "unduly burdensome" include waiting periods, parental consent mandates, counseling materials slanted toward carrying a pregnancy to term, laws against taking a minor across state lines to obtain an abortion, and bans on insurance paying for abortions for low-income women or women in the military.

There is ample evidence that such restrictions, particularly in the aggregate, create daunting obstacles for some women, particularly the poor and the young. Only seven states (California, Connecticut, Hawaii, New

York, Oregon, Vermont, and Washington) and the District of Columbia have almost no restrictions. Moreover, it is clear that the phrase "undue burden" is itself open to widely varying interpretations. For example, in 2000, the Supreme Court ruled by a vote of 5-4, in *Stenberg v. Carhart*, that states could not ban the D&X (dilation and extraction) abortion method without allowing an exception to protect the life *or* health of the woman. On April 18, 2007, a similar case was decided by the Court quite differently, reflecting the addition of two Bush appointees, Justice Samuel Alito and Chief Justice John Roberts. That day, the Supreme Court upheld the Partial-Birth Abortion Ban Act, which made the Intact Dilation and Evacuation (or D&E) abortion method illegal except to save the life of the mother. This marked the first time *any* medical procedure was banned, as well as the first time an exception for a woman's health had been overruled.

Restrictions, ironically, contribute to later abortions and more need for procedures such as the D&E—as women rarely change their minds about having procedures just because they are forced to jump through hoops. "It's so incredibly insulting," Dr. Susan Wicklund said in a 2007 interview in the *New York Times*. "The twenty-four-hour waiting period implies that women don't think about it on their own and have to have the government forcing it on them. To me, a lot of the abortion restrictions are about control of women, about power, and it's insulting."

Provider Shortage

For the last decade, eighty-seven percent of counties in the U.S. haven't had any abortion providers, which means that about one-third of women aged fifteen to forty-four live in areas without this service. Many medical schools do not require training in abortion techniques, even if students are going into OB/GYN or family practice. Despite the rise of groups like Medical Students for Choice (currently 10,000 members strong), physicians do not necessarily support their colleagues who provide procedures. "Only with abortion do doctors make referrals without even the courtesy of a call to the doctor who will be performing the abortion," says Dr. Morris Wortman, a provider in Rochester, New York, in the film *On Hostile Ground*.

There are fewer doctors willing and able to do procedures, and there are fewer places in which they can be performed. Clinics affiliated with the Catholic Church, for instance, have been buying secular hospital systems and banning services such as abortions, birth control, tubal ligations, vasectomies, and emergency contraception for rape victims.

Pro-choicers had hoped that medical abortion—mifepristone, the American version of the RU-486 abortion pill—would help make up for the lack of providers. A 2005 survey undertaken by the Guttmacher Institute indicated that some doctors who didn't provide surgical procedures as part of their practices were offering medical abortions, slowing (but not reversing) the decline in providers. (However, medical abortion hasn't expanded the geographic area of abortion services, as was hoped.) Unfortunately, FDA restrictions and the high cost (in time and money) of providing this option have meant that, thus far, it is not being used by many doctors who didn't already provide surgical abortions. However, continuing efforts to engage and provide training to doctors about medical abortion are under way.

Money

Procedures are *rarely* covered by state Medicaid or insurance, due to the aforementioned Hyde Amendment. Federal Medicaid can only pay in cases of rape, incest, or if the woman's life is in danger. As of April 1, 2008, only seventeen states choose to fund abortions via state Medicaid: Alaska, Arizona, California, Connecticut, Hawaii, Illinois, Maryland, Massachusetts, Minnesota, Montana, New Jersey, New Mexico, New York, Oregon, Vermont, Washington, and West Virginia. Two in five, or thirty-nine percent (5.4 million), of American women of reproductive age depend on Medicaid for their health coverage. Medicaid pays for two of every five births (thirty-nine percent). A first-trimester abortion costs on average around $350. Some fifty-eight percent of abortions occur within the first eight weeks, while eighty-nine percent occur within the first twelve weeks (Centers for Disease Control, 2000). A second-trimester abortion—eleven percent of procedures occur within the thirteenth to twentieth week—usually runs about $1,200 to $1,800. This can be an impossible fee if you are poor or a teenager, the two populations most likely to have later abortions.

Antiabortion Terrorism

In recent decades, an active network of extremists has murdered seven people and attempted to kill seventeen others. There have been more than 5,800 reported instances of violence against clinics and their workers since 1977, according to the National Abortion Federation. Heavily targeted clinics must ramp up security on their own dime—costs that can reach $25,000 to $100,000 annually. The last few years have seen a decline in clinic violence—knock on wood—as a more female-centered pro-life movement has emerged, led by women such as Abstinence Clearinghouse's Leslee Unruh and Feminists for Life of America's Serrin M. Foster.

ACTIVISM VS. TERRORISM

All of the deterrents or roadblocks, including restrictive laws and lack of providers, have some root in the organized antiabortion movement. Antichoice or pro-life activists were energized by *Roe* in 1973, but began gaining higher visibility in the 1980s and especially the 1990s. They have the luxury to work more vociferously on their activist messages, too, because they don't tend to provide any services. They don't provide Pap smears or abortions, obviously, nor do they provide contraception, prenatal health care, or childcare, despite a clear connection to their mandate.

The antichoice movement has not yet been able to end legalized abortion, but has undermined it in many ways. One of the most recent tactics is to sue clinics for not disclosing the "link" between having an abortion and an increased risk of breast cancer. (There is not, in fact, a link—at least not according the National Cancer Institute, the American Cancer Society, or major research universities.) The movement also publicizes "post-abortion syndrome," which posits that women feel debilitating shock and depression after an abortion. Nada L. Stotland, MD, president-elect of the American Psychiatric Association refuted this in a May 28, 2007 letter to the *New York Times*, writing that "meticulous research shows that there is no causal relationship between abortions and mental illnesses. Women's mental health is jeopardized when laws require doctors to mislead them and is best served when women make their own decisions. That's why the American Psychiatric Association stands in favor of women's access to reproductive health care."

As lobbyists and as a media presence, the conservative arm of the right-to-life movement is quite influential. This wasn't always the case. But in 1980, the Moral Majority (an ultra-right religious organization then headed by Jerry Falwell) helped Ronald Reagan win the White House. To date, antichoice groups such as the National Right to Life Committee and Operation Rescue/ Operation Save America exert considerable power within the conservative wing of the Republican Party. This relationship was made clear when President George W. Bush reinstated the antichoice Mexico City Policy (also known as the "global gag rule") as the first action of his presidency. (President Clinton had dismantled it in 1993 as the first action of his presidency.) This policy bans any international organizations—including those providing crucial women's health care in impoverished regions—from providing or even discussing abortion, as a condition for receiving any U.S. government funding.

The terrorist networks related to antichoice extremists—which resort to stalking, firebombing clinics, and murder—must be differentiated from the organized antichoice movement exercising freedom of speech. Still, there is ample evidence that the more radical wings of the movement provide cover and support for the terrorist factions. Perhaps nobody could have anticipated the violence, but once it began happening, police and government officials entrusted with protecting women and clinicians were slow to treat the antichoice attacks as terrorism.

As forward-thinking and free as U.S. society has typically been, abortion is one of the least protected rights we have. It's easier to buy a gun in many states (no need for waiting periods or background checks or counseling) than it is to get this medical procedure. Following the terrorist attacks of September 11, 2001, abortion providers were struck with a sick recognition: They had already been receiving death threats from fundamentalists on a regular basis. Innocent people had been murdered and stalked, letters that claimed to contain anthrax had been sent. (In fact, abortion clinics have long had policies in place to deal with these eventualities). Then, in the weeks following the destruction of the World Trade Center towers, at least five hundred more pieces of mail said to contain anthrax arrived at abortion clinics.

By November 2001, however, the FBI had elevated the attacks on reproductive health providers from hate crimes to domestic terrorism. This built upon some protective measures already in place, such as the Federal Access to Clinic Entrances (FACE) Act of 1994, which created federal penalties for obstructing entrances to reproductive health centers and for harassing those who work there.

The debates around abortion are fueled by the most profound political and personal issues. On an individual level, abortion usually intersects with a woman's self-image, her relationship with her family, her religion, and her sex life. Politically, abortion impacts our views of sexuality, gender roles, power, and control over human reproduction. In many ways, people line up on this issue from either a fundamentalist or progressive worldview. While many pro-choice people are religious, they tend to separate sex from procreation. Religious fundamentalists do not. Thus, pro-life activism is often not about abortion; it is about a whole range of human rights and values. Operation Rescue/Operation Save America, for example, wants to combat "teen sex, homosexuality, and the absence of God from the classroom," too.

A softer version of this philosophy is apparent in the abstinence or virginity movement. Since the mid-'90s, more than 2.5 million young people have taken "virginity pledges," often through the program True Love Waits or the more MTV-style dance party Silver Ring Thing; more than a billion federal dollars has been fed to "abstinence only" endeavors (including the Abstinence Clearinghouse and Silver Ring Thing) since the Adolescent Family Life Act was passed in 1981.

Although the motive of some antichoice activists is to cultivate violence and fear, others promote values that include abolishing the death penalty, vegetarianism, and other life-affirming political stands. Some antichoice activists consider themselves to be feminists and are attempting to be authentically pro-life. The group Feminists for Life of America was founded to bridge a pro-woman philosophy with pro-life politics. They say they want to both provide resources to support women who want to bring their pregnancies to term *and* fight exploitation of women.

Some pro-life women also fear what pro-choice activists fear: that young women and low-income women sometimes "choose" abortion because they feel they have no other options. For instance, a Milwaukee clinic I visited in 2001 reported a rise in clients saying they felt they "needed" to have an abortion after welfare was dismantled in the mid-1990s. A woman getting an abortion because she fears she won't have adequate support to raise the child is not what is meant by "reproductive freedom." In fact, the emerging movement for reproductive justice is equally concerned with providing support for women who choose to have children. When antichoice activists are simply co-opting the roots and language of the abortion rights movement, they aren't feminists. Working to take a choice away from other women can never be construed as feminist, pro-woman, or even pro-life—given the deaths of women we know occur when abortion is illegal. But those who are actively finding ways to create options for women who don't want to have abortions (yet who need childcare and other forms of assistance) can honorably use the term *pro-life feminist*. Given how few resources there are for poor women and women with disabilities who want to keep their children, these activists can find common cause with activists for reproductive freedom and justice.

Some of the abortion rights movement's potential is in making itself obsolete—not through harassment and criminalization, but through user-friendly birth control and honest sex education. About half of the nearly six million U.S. pregnancies per year are accidents. This rate is two to five times higher than that of other industrialized nations. If trends continue, abortions *will* be less common in the future—but only if comprehensive, responsible sex education and access to contraceptives and family planning remain available. We can look to Western Europe—where abortion is funded, accessible, and less frequent—to see how this works.

In 1994, women of color working for abortion rights put forth a theory, strategy, and practice called "reproductive justice" that described a paradigm shift for the future. According to the SisterSong Women of Color Reproductive Health Collective, reproductive justice is a concise set of three human rights that allow a woman to: 1) decide if and when she will have a baby and the conditions under which she will give birth; 2) consider her options for preventing or ending a pregnancy; and 3) parent the children she has with the necessary social supports in safe environments and healthy communities, and without fear of violence from individuals or the government.

For three decades, abortion access has been predicated on privacy rights, which emphasize keeping the government from intruding on our daily lives. The human rights–based framework advocated by SisterSong enables an affirmative role for the government to make sure that abortion is actually safe, legal, affordable, and accessible. Ironically, while the term "reproductive justice" is gaining mainstream currency, groups like SisterSong are still not being fully engaged in meaningfully implementing the strategy. As Loretta Ross of SisterSong put it to me, "Reproductive justice acknowledges that the ability of anyone to make a decision about her body depends on what community she is in, and which human rights violations are acting on that community."

The United States is a nation with great potential for egalitarian ideals, and yet the human rights of women are still a work in progress. If we look at SisterSong's message as a roadmap for the next three decades, perhaps we will discover a nation whose reality matches that of its rhetoric.

CHAPTER 2

THE "I HAD AN ABORTION" PROJECT

My sister's abortion in the fall of 1985 was a profound moment for me. She was sixteen, I was fifteen, and she came to me for help in raising the $200 that she needed, choosing not to go to my pro-choice parents and risk having them see her in a "different light"—that is, as a daughter who was sexual. Finding that money on a short deadline and bringing it to her on my bike to the local clinic, the only one in the whole state, was one of the first times I realized I truly had the power to help some-one else.

Nearly two decades later, in the fall of 2003, I was finishing up a book on grassroots activism with my writing partner Amy Richards, living in my studio on downtown New York City's Avenue B, and attempting to break up with my boyfriend, when I had a sudden brainstorm. The big march on Washington for abortion rights was scheduled for a few months later, in April 2004. I had attended the 1992 march as a college student and recalled that people donned shirts with in-your-face messages like, *George, Get Out of My Bush!* I decided I would make a T-shirt (hundreds of them) that said, simply, *I had an abortion*—which struck me as both quiet and yet the boldest message one could brandish. (I didn't intend to wear it myself, since I felt it should be a truthful admission, as opposed to a symbolic gesture.)

My friend Sandy once told me she wanted to make a shirt that conveyed her biggest secret, which in her case was her abortion during college in Montreal. I thought of my sister, whose abortion years before was still something she felt people could use against her to demonstrate that she wasn't a good person. I (like others) wanted to put a face on this divisive issue, to encourage women to come out, and to demonstrate that abortion wasn't something that ignorant, heartless people went through—that, in fact, the women who'd had abortions were our mothers, sisters, grandmothers, daughters, and best friends. In 1971, prominent French women had signed a manifesto declaring that they'd had illegal abortions. The next year, the first issue of Ms. magazine featured a similar campaign, which was reprised by the magazine in 2006.

I discussed the T-shirts with a group of feminists who had begun their activism in the '70s and who reminded me that their stories of abortion—unapologetic, often totally free of trauma or emotions other than relief—were never represented in the mainstream press. Some of them suggested that the shirts should read: "I had an abortion. I'm not sorry"—the latter portion inspired by Patricia Beninato's website imnotsorry.net. Initially, I agreed with that, but after reaching out beyond that group of women—to my sister, my friends, my mother's friends—I learned that while no one I spoke with quite regretted their decision, few felt comfortable with the phrase, *I'm not sorry*. It sounded petulant, said one trusted friend; callous, said another. So, I committed to making shirts that made a simple, factual statement without editorializing. The Third Wave Foundation agreed to front the printing costs; my friend Erin Wade designed the shirt for free.

Meanwhile, I focused on making a film of women's abortion stories. I had been interviewed for dozens of documentaries over the years but had no clue how to make one myself or what it might cost. A close friend, Gillian Aldrich, is a talented producer who had worked for years with arguably the most successful documentary filmmaker of all time: Michael Moore. Gillian had also just given birth to a baby, and a few years before that she'd had an abortion with the man who later became her husband and father of her children. I asked Gillian if she'd make the film with me and what it might cost. She said she could do a bare-bones ten-minute video for $3,500—but "no sound mix, no archival footage, and no color correction for that," she added. That's okay, I assured her, I had no idea what those things were, anyway.

With a similar spirit to when I had raised money for my sister's abortion all those years earlier by figuring out who could give me a quick $200, I thought about who in my life might be able to financially support the project. I wrote a mission letter, which read in part:

> *Women raised post–Roe v. Wade have lived in a world in which abortion was a legal entitlement, should we seek one. But the guilt and silence around having an abortion hasn't dissipated. The stories of abortion that are most circulated are negative; sensational accounts of botched and traumatic procedures that aren't representative of the 1.3 million terminations that occur in the U.S. each year. I Had an Abortion is a documentary that seeks to counter these distortions. In encouraging women to tell their stories, we hope to demonstrate that women might have complex, or even painful, experiences with abortion, but they are still grateful to have had access to the procedure—very, very grateful. The film reflects the voices that typically go unheard in this loud debate, deepening our understanding of why we support abortion rights.*

In search of the $3,500 Gillian assessed as our budget, I sent the letter to my mother's friends in our hometown of Fargo; after all, most had some discretionary income and had always been supportive of me. I was scared, though, because while these family friends knew the sort of issues I cared about, in many cases I had never discussed abortion with them directly. What if I offended them? Was I being hopelessly presumptuous? Would I become the laughing stock of Fargo?

Within a week of sending the letter, I received more than twenty responses, most very encouraging and most sending checks between $50 and $100. The one critical letter helped me to rejigger the project a bit to more clearly convey that I was looking for honest experiences of abortion and wasn't afraid to hear that some people had regrets. I wrote back to that friend thanking her for her frankness and received another letter from her thanking me for being open to criticism; in it, she included a check.

The process of raising money for the film forced me to practice what I was encouraging others to do. I realized that I was still afraid to discuss abortion in polite company. By being direct and humble (yet very cognizant of how emotional this topic is for people), I found that my hometown of Fargo, which I had always imagined was super-conservative, was filled with thoughtful, supportive, dedicated people who were, in many cases, much more radical than I.

Dozens of older feminists, mainly those on the History in Action listserv, also ponied up checks ranging from $10 to $30 (along with insight and direction). Katha Pollitt wrote about the project in her column in the *Nation* magazine, and dozens more checks arrived. Soon, we had the requisite $3,500. In addition to the financial support, I began collecting stories from hundreds of women and more than a few men, many of whom said that they had never shared their experiences with anyone. One story, from Mary Fox, began:

My daughter told me you were looking for stories about abortion. I had mine in 1978 in Oakland. I already had three children, ages nine, seven, and five, and was living with a domineering and abusive (only mental and emotional at the time) man, father of my youngest. His idea of birth control was none . . .

Another woman, Paige Tensch, explained:

I got pregnant at seventeen; the first time I ever had sex. My family was strong Southern Baptists and my mother cried every time she tried to talk about sex. I didn't know then that my parents had a terrible relationship and thought of divorce but felt they could not break their marriage vows . . .

Women told me about their illegal abortions, including this letter from Janet Grant:

> *I went to an abortionist in Tijuana, Mexico about whom I had heard good things. His office was clean, not elegant, but not dissimilar to one in the U.S. Suddenly the five of us in the waiting room were told that we needed to leave immediately. It was a police raid—they probably hadn't been paid off that month. We were herded into a big car and driven out into the countryside. On a rise there was a pink stucco house. A boy of ten opened a garage door and closed it after we got out of the car and entered the "alternative clinic." A sixteen-year-old girl was sobbing on my shoulder and all of us were apprehensive. The room [where we had our abortions] was a converted kitchen, immaculate, and well-equipped . . .*

Women like Rachel Ida Buff told me about their later-term abortions: "I had a twenty-six-week abortion in the Wichita clinic because we were told that there was grave impairment to the fetus, our second child. It was a wrenching and difficult decision, but one about which I have no regrets. I am now nine months, healthily, pregnant with another child."

They told me about their multiple abortions: "I am forty years old and I have had five abortions, one miscarriage, and two children," wrote a woman in Oakland, California. "It sounds astounding, even to me."

Women like Gail Coufal wrote about how relieved they were for any avenue to talk about their abortions:

> *Having had two abortions at very different times/stages in my life, and having kept the Great Secret from most of my extremely Catholic family, I've often yearned for this very outlet, especially to hear other women's stories. My life is not perfect, I have struggled with health issues; but I have never been sorry for the choices I made not to have children. My parents both died last year and I wonder if the moratorium for family secrets is over now?*

In all, I received well over one hundred stories. I already had a list of dozens of friends and acquaintances whose stories I thought would be good, ranging from women's rights leaders Gloria Steinem, Byllye Avery, and Loretta Ross to friends like Amy Richards and Dawn Lundy Martin. Gillian interviewed nineteen women, I interviewed two, and we made two interviewing trips jointly (one to San Francisco and the other to Detroit) to get three more stories. The end result was a film that was (painfully) whittled down by Gillian, myself, and editor Kristen Nutile to ten moving stories. It begins with Florence Rice, who had an abortion in 1938, moves to A'yen Tran, who had her second abortion in 2003, and concludes with dozens of women looking in the camera and saying, "I had an abortion." During the many times I have seen the film since it began screening around the world on January 22, 2005, I often cry at the women's vulnerability and courage to say those words openly to the world.

While working on the film, I became accidentally pregnant. By the time of the April 2004 March for Women's Lives, I was nearly five months along. On the July evening when the Drudge Report first posted a provocative item about the *I had an abortion* T-shirts, I was seven months pregnant, and my swelling belly felt like a buffer between me and the crazed hate mail I was receiving in the wake of the shirt controversy. Media from CNN and Fox News to the *Atlanta Journal-Constitution* to *Glamour* magazine to Rush Limbaugh ran stories, and the shirt sold out immediately. (See the Appendix for a great essay from *Bitch* magazine that analyzes what so provoked many on the prochoice side to react negatively to both the shirt and Planned Parenthood's decision to sell them.)

Gillian and I began touring with the film (which eventually expanded to fifty-five minutes and cost $40,000 to complete), speaking to Democratic women's groups in New Mexico, Planned Parenthoods in upstate New York, and college students in Minnesota. Men always attended and often requested that we make a film documenting their experiences, which are even more suppressed. One evening, after a rough cut of the film had been shown in my hometown at the enormous Fargo Theatre (*I Had an Abortion* resplendent on the art deco marquee) and Gillian and I entered the venue, startled at the presence of dozens of protesters, a man stood up shakily during the Q and A. "I am a youth minister in Fargo," he began, glancing nervously at his seatmates, "and I'm pro-life. I came here to protest and I want to tell you that . . ." He paused and looked at his fellow protesters. "I wanted to tell you that I learned something tonight. I had never thought of the woman's side, I had never heard a story from a woman who had that experience, and I felt compassion. So thank you for that."

Gillian and I were trembling after he spoke, because we had never really had such a human, direct, non-platitudinous conversation with someone who identified as pro-life; we were humbled that he had come to our event and was brave enough to say that the stories of women touched him. I was learning that despite working for reproductive rights since I was a teenager escorting patients into the local clinic while the Lambs of Christ protested outside, there was still a lot I didn't understand. My esteem for the pro-choice activists and clinic-workers was understandable, but I began to look at the world beyond their everyday heroism as I considered abortion. I started allowing myself to understand what is true for me: that I think of pregnancy as "life" but this doesn't have to mean that abortion is murder.

Gillian, meanwhile, was having her own journey: "Doing the film changed me," she says. "It took abortion from a knee-jerk political position I had and allowed me to see these stories for what they are—as parts of life, not political decisions. It was very, very liberating to not have to pigeonhole, to find each interview more complex than the next—and to just let them be that way."

The abortion stories of each era were so different, but Gillian and I both came to appreciate that, throughout history, every major advance in reproductive freedom was preceded by women telling the truth about their lives. Around the turn of the century, Margaret Sanger shed light on the women who were dying early and miserable deaths due to a lack of contraception and near-constant childbearing; this helped to usher in birth control. We hoped that women telling their stories now—when abortion is legal but still so stigmatized that it's rarely discussed openly—could launch a new arm of the struggle. Women (and men) can personalize what has become a vicious and abstract debate. We can sit together and learn from one another, drawing from the unguarded, personal shades of people's lives, rather than the black-and-white, aggressive rhetoric of opposing sides.

We've done this before, we feminists. In 1969, feminists drew from their own lives and risked telling the truth about their abortions—this marked the beginning of the repeal of abortion laws. These stories were often harrowing. Some women were forced to carry their pregnancies but then coerced into giving their babies up for adoption—the babies literally taken from their arms after their signatures were procured. Other women had to pay extortion-level prices for their procedures or endure shady, molesting men—who even knew if the guy was a doctor?—who performed their abortions. Some women died from their illegal procedures. And many women were treated with great compassion by people who risked their careers and home lives to help—such as the famed Dr. Robert Spencer, who performed more than 40,000 safe, illegal abortions in the mining region of Pennsylvania before his death in 1969.

Why are these stories so important? Because a story is not a debate, it doesn't have sides. Unlike an argument or a slogan, a story can be as complex as a woman's life. Listening to women's abortion stories today serves a dual purpose: It reflects the urgency of abortion rights and, if we are listening and if we are creative, it indicates places where the movement needs to go.

CHAPTER 3

THE RISE OF PRO-VOICE

Aspen Baker was born in a trailer on the beach in San Diego on January 22, 1976, the third anniversary of *Roe v. Wade*. Her parents were "surfers, but surfing Christians," says Baker, who was home-schooled. Her mother was a former Catholic, and Baker was raised in a non-denominational Christian church. Baker was pro-choice, sort of, but she also knew that she could never have an abortion herself. "I didn't imagine that I would ever get pregnant and not want to be," says Baker. "And certainly the idea of taking off my clothes, getting up on a table, and having someone go into my vagina and take out something growing in my uterus did not sound good to me." She considered herself a responsible person and, at the time, "my thought was that the responsible decision would be to have a baby if I became pregnant."

In 1999, just after she graduated from Berkeley, though, she learned she *was* pregnant. "Initially, I believed I was going to be a mother and have the baby," she says, but her situation was precarious. She was living with room-mates, working as a bartender—"Imagine the eight-months-pregnant bartender," she laughs—and she sensed that the relationship she was in was short term; she would be a single mom. Two coworkers at the bar told her that they'd had abortions and felt it was the right choice. While Baker gradually realized that she didn't want to have the baby, the decision to actually have an abortion was very hard on her. "If I think that having the baby is the responsible choice, then what does this abortion say about me?" she wondered.

"When I finally went, it was in a hospital, and I had a nice doctor who explained the procedure to me and plenty of counseling beforehand," she recounts. "I was so grateful for the positive medical experience, despite my ambivalence." She assumed that at some point, however, someone at the clinic was going to tell her about follow-up counseling. But no one did. "I didn't bring it up myself because if it's not something that they do, then I figured that my feelings were abnormal and would go away," she says.

They didn't. In fact, her confusion and sadness only increased. "I thought I'd never have an abortion—and now I had. I questioned my moral beliefs as a human rights activist. I didn't believe in the death penalty. I felt bad about the boyfriend, who had gotten back with his ex." When she told her parents, who were divorced, her mother quickly got off the phone. "I'm really close to my father, and when I told him, he cried all night and told me that this was something I would have to 'reveal' to my husband someday . . . I cried all of the time, but I didn't want to burden my friends."

Fortunately, her father called her back the day after that initial phone call. He told her he loved her, that he wanted to support her any way he could, he just hadn't known what to do in the moment. Baker realized that she and her father actually needed some help with the aftermath of what had turned out to be a profound experience. She began looking for after-abortion resources—and looking and looking. All she could find to offer support were thinly disguised antiabortion groups. As a feminist, she says, "I didn't see anything that reflected my experience" of having sad feelings around her abortion, but not wanting to make abortion illegal. Seeking resolution, she interned at NARAL Pro-Choice California, an arm one of the country's oldest abortion rights organizations. But when she would raise the issue of the lack of emotional resources for women, she was confronted with blank faces. It was, she says, as if admitting that she was struggling with her feelings meant that she wasn't really pro-choice.

Eventually, Baker met several like-minded women (Carolina De Robertis, Anna Goldstein, Susan Criscione, and Laura Perez) and in 2000, sitting on the floor in one of their apartments, they created Exhale, a nonjudgmental post-abortion talkline. The group tried to eliminate anything in their outreach materials that might stop a woman from calling, including words like "feminist" and "pro-choice," even though Exhale is both. "We didn't know if we'd ever get a call," Baker remembers. "But we got our first call the second night. It was from a father who wanted to know how to support his daughter." In 2007, Exhale created a series of Hallmark-like e-cards that people could send to loved ones who'd had abortions—not to celebrate the abortion, but to acknowledge it and offer comfort. By 2008, Exhale was available nationwide, seven days a week, in multiple languages, with an annual budget of $300,000. Of the five hundred calls they receive each month, around ten percent are from men, often wanting to know what they can do to help a daughter or partner going through an abortion.

Exhale's founders are part of a growing group of primarily young abortion supporters who believe that the way we practice and talk about unplanned pregnancy and termination has to evolve, or else we risk alienating more women, including those who've had abortion experiences. They aren't traditionally political—Exhale's work doesn't address legal rights or host lobbying days—but they are radically feminist in ideology.

The same is true for the Haven Coalition, a hosting network in New York City founded in 2001 by Catherine Megill. Haven provides places to stay for women who travel long distances to have later-term abortions (and thus two- and three-day procedures) in the city. Hosts are vetted to weed out both pro-life and pro-choice proselytizers.

This shift in focus in the national conversation from "Keep your laws off my body!" to "Let's talk about feelings and whether fetal life has value" has been tough for the pro-choice movement to acknowledge, given the nonstop hostility from protesters and antiabortion politicians, and the experience of a pioneering clinic director named Charlotte Taft is illuminating in this regard.

In 1980, two years into her tenure directing the Routh Street abortion clinic in Dallas, Taft decided to draw up a questionnaire for patients coming in for their two-week checkups. "I wanted to know if patients were afraid to be intimate sexually and emotionally after a procedure and did they feel adequately protected from another unintended pregnancy—so I asked a lot of open-ended questions," recalls Taft, now fifty-eight and a counselor in private practice in Glorieta, New Mexico. "I was shocked by how many who seemed fine during the procedure were now having thoughts and feelings that no one had anticipated. They wondered, *How can I feel sad about something I chose?*"

Often they felt like they couldn't talk to their partners about the feelings, even if their partners were supportive of the choice. It ran counter to everything Taft knew: Women came to a clinic in crisis, she had assumed, and they left relieved—pure and simple. While it was, in her estimation, just seven to ten percent of her patients who needed the follow-up care, when you are talking about more than a million procedures in the U.S. each year, "that ends up being a lot of people," she notes. Abortion patients get more pre-counseling than those undergoing any other medical procedure—and still, Taft found, it was not safe for women to talk about abortion in their lives. "Number one, it was supposed to be a secret," says Taft. "So these women had no idea who else in their lives had gone through this experience. Two, we don't have good language even today for making a good but complex decision. Third, some women felt that if they said anything, it was ammunition to remove the right to choose. You either said you were fine or admitted you were a murderer."

Around that same time, in 1981, Peg Johnston was opening Southern Tier Women's Services, an independent abortion clinic near Binghamton, New York. "I came out of a rape crisis background," says Johnston, now sixty. "Back then, rape was really controversial. People didn't believe that it was a problem." A red diaper baby and the grand-niece of a suffragist, Elizabeth Freeman, Johnston had grown up with radical ideas and developed a reputation as someone who could handle controversy. And she got it: Five years after the Southern Tier clinic opened, fellow Binghamton resident Randall Terry founded what would become the nation's most notorious antiabortion organization, Operation Rescue, and pioneered his strategy of blocking clinic entrances at Johnston's practice. Johnston kept her sense of humor, counter-picketing Operation Rescue and posting a sign outside the clinic that read, *Please Don't Feed the Protesters.*

After a while, though, Johnston began turning her attention from the protesters. "I don't know if I just started getting bored with Operation Rescue, but I definitely started to get interested in what women were saying instead," she recalls. She'd hear a protester chant, "You're killing your baby!" and then she'd sit in a counseling session with a woman who'd say, "I feel like I'm killing my baby." At first, she assumed that the patients were simply repeating what they'd heard outside, having internalized right-wing disinformation that Johnston needed to "correct." "Once I began listening more intently to her," she now admits, "I learned that she *wasn't* saying what the picketer was saying—although she used the same words." Johnston believes that women were genuinely struggling with the value of life and how to do the right thing and be a good person, just as Aspen Baker reported feeling. "Frequently they were already mothers and they knew a time when, at that same stage of pregnancy, they had welcomed the life and felt like it was their baby. They weren't mouthing an antichoice message, they were acknowledging that this was serious stuff—*How can I want one kid and not the other?* I felt like they needed a place to say the worst and then work their way to the rightness of their decision. Some were on a journey to realize the power and responsibility of being a mother," says Johnston. "Which is that sometimes it's the power of saying no to a life."

Truly listening to everything a patient has to say—and letting them use words like "loss" and "baby" and "killing"—is one of a number of relatively recent innovations among cutting-edge abortion activists, mainly those operating within geographic locales where abortion is not acceptable. (My critique, it must be noted, is coming from a woman living in a nation that has known nearly four decades of meaningful abortion rights. Some of what I'm suggesting would be less relevant in countries with emerging abortion rights movement. The U.S. can't remain in the same rhetorical place it was in the '70s, or even the '80s—we are in a position where we must evolve.)

Some of the philosophical foremothers of this group—including Charlotte Taft, Peg Johnston, and others—call themselves the November Gang. They are a combination think tank and support group named after the month in 1989 when they first met in response to the Supreme Court's *Webster v. Reproductive Health Services* decision. *Webster* upheld a Missouri statute banning the use of public facilities and other state resources for abortions and codified that most restrictions were fine as long as they weren't *too* onerous for a woman. In other words, she might have to jump through many hoops on the way to the abortion—from mandatory delays to having to sell her car in order to pay for the procedure—but as long as she could jump, the hoops weren't in conflict with *Roe v. Wade*. According to Johnston, the group's mission is to "explore the work abortion providers are doing" simply by providing a space for the clinic directors to talk openly about their fears and observations. At first Taft and Johnston focused on defense outside of clinics: *Will Roe stand? How much are we spending on security?* But after a while, they began to discuss what happened *within* the clinic. And they started asking questions that shocked some of their colleagues. *What if we show fetal tissue to patients when they want to see it? Why are we protecting ourselves from what the patients are really saying? What do you do if a patient wants to baptize the remains?*

Many of the clinicians do indeed offer to show fetal tissue to patients, and viewing it is often a relief to the woman. My sister accompanied me to the clinic in Fargo where she'd had her abortion some twenty years earlier, and was surprised to see how undeveloped an eleven-week fetus is. "I had pictured something else all of these years," she told me. I, however, was taken aback upon discovering that a fetus at younger than ten weeks has perfectly formed hands and feet, just like the pro-life poster with the tiny hand on the dime leads you to believe. At the clinic, I was intrigued by the journals that the staff left in the waiting and recovery rooms in which patients could jot down thoughts. Many women wrote some version of, *Don't think of it as losing a baby, but as gaining a guardian angel.* These were women who clearly felt relationships to their pregnancies as children, not as masses of cells. They were choosing not to have that baby right now, but in many cases, there was ambivalence and loss in the decision.

Charlotte Taft identifies a 1995 Naomi Wolf essay from the *New Republic* called "Our Bodies, Our Souls" as the first time she saw these ideas spoken in the feminist mainstream. Wolf's essay called for the pro-choice movement to embrace guilt and acknowledge that some women mourn the loss of their fetuses. Wolf also wrote movingly of the conversion from pro-choice to pro-life of one Norma McCorvey—Jane Roe. At the time of that essay's publication, I was an editor at *Ms.* and Wolf's take was very controversial in the office, to say the least. I felt she was handing ammunition to the right wing and condescending to abortion rights activists—did she think we didn't contemplate moral issues? I didn't know what to make of McCorvey.

After having spent the last several years talking to women about their abortion stories, I am embarrassed by the knee-jerk naïvete I had back then. Today, I'd say that talking honestly about abortion is a sign of the movement's strength—and it's a feminist act. On the one hand, it's true that some women experience their abortions as empowering—such as my friend whose procedure nearly forty years ago meant that she could accept a Fulbright scholarship—and that you rarely, if ever, hear those stories in the media. But for people with no money, chaotic relationships, tense marriages, too many kids already, drug and alcohol issues, or abusive partners, an abortion might be the right thing to do "yet certainly also evidence of a life they wish they weren't leading," as a friend trenchantly put it. Abortion might be a way of taking charge of your life, but for younger women, who often know plenty about birth control, needing one can make you feel that you wouldn't be in this predicament if you really did have control of your life.

Merle Hoffman responded in *On the Issues* to Naomi Wolf's article, writing that "McCorvey reflects the ambivalence, the struggles, and the daily untidiness of existence . . . She has all the debris and baggage of a difficult and hard-lived life. Her class separates her from the leadership of the movement just as her outlaw nature does . . . In the end she is still alone, and that is the greatest failing of the pro-choice movement's behavior towards her. It's not that it did not offer her salvation or absolution. It did not even offer her sisterhood."

Hoffman found Wolf's analysis too simplistic, but as a woman who has witnessed thousands of abortions in her three-plus decades running the Choices Women's Medical Center in Queens, she knows that many of the millions of women who have actually had abortions since legalization "share much of the baggage McCorvey carried. Some are ambivalent and embarrassed. Others search for comfort and validation. The leadership's failure to embrace [patients'] reality and the movement's other core constituency, the providers who actually make abortion possible, leave both vulnerable to attack and harassment." Nearly ten years after Naomi Wolf's controversial essay, a firestorm erupted around an article by Frances Kissling, the former president of Catholics for a Free Choice. Kissling's suggestion that a healthy society values life, including fetal life, remains divisive among advocates.

Some might argue that it is a sensitive (or wrong-headed) moment to acknowledge the emotions around abortion and the fetus, since supporters of abortion rights have been losing legislative ground while the pro-life world has seen many years of unparalleled mainstream political support, including being commended by President Bush for their work each year on the *Roe* anniversary. Meanwhile, the threat that legal abortion could be overturned has animated most strategic discussions of choice for the past three decades and accounts for the brittle and defensive posture of the abortion rights side.

Abortion clinics have had an undeniably positive impact on medical care in this country. The concepts of outpatient surgery in general and free-standing surgery centers have grown out of the marginalized world of abortion; the idea that a health professional should talk to patients and provide counseling was based on abortion provision. But "everything conspires to make it so that the clinics must provide services in a war zone," as Hoffman puts it. "There is constant harassment, vendors refusing to work with the clinic, constant threats of eviction, roadblocks to getting insurance, the unending nuisance of malpractice litigation." This has all taken a toll on providers. Within that challenging environment, some continue to function well, and others pass the stress of antagonism onto the client. Because of some state-level bills mandating that clinics read warnings about the "risks" of abortion or show patients their ultrasounds, counseling and medical care are often forced into a script.

Of course, all clinics have women's emotional health in mind even as their priority is offering safe medical care. The problem is, for many clinics, the gap between their stated values and the clinic experience they have created. Because of violence at some clinics and the constant threats that staff members face as they attempt to do their jobs, many clinic workers have been programmed, in a sense, by the "antis" to respond reflexively to women's emotions. These workers have at times become barriers to patients being able to get information or emotional support—almost viewing the need for after-abortion care as caving into the antichoice forces alleging that women are permanently damaged by abortion. For instance, I have been in several clinics where the state mandates that patients be read a list of potential hazards of abortion. Because there is controversy as to whether these "warnings" have any validity, I have seen clinic workers express their frustration by reading the statement really quickly and all but rolling their eyes. It's not a scenario that invites the patient to ask any questions or express any fears. What should be an entry point for communication with the patient is diverted into a complaint about imposed restrictions. In order to make sure that women who need care get it, pro-voice initiatives spearheaded by Exhale and the November Gang (and others) state that 1) everyone deserves access to the information, and 2) offering emotional resources and information doesn't imply that everyone is (or should be) having problems.

Emily Barcklow is a young woman who, like Aspen Baker, never knew a time when abortion wasn't legal. She had an abortion when she was nineteen and attending Evergreen State College. "It was not an easy decision," she recalls. "I struggled with feelings of deviance, selfishness, and loss afterwards." Four years, lots of counseling, and an "amazing ritual process" helped her feel resolved. But at a NARAL event on the University of Washington campus in 2001, Barcklow spent hours preparing a presentation about her experience and closure ritual. "I arrived at the speak-out and was disappointed with the lack of depth in the other presentations—all recycled coat hangers and *We'll never go back* signs. I would cite this experience as my first real disconnect from the mainstream abortion rights movement." Barcklow eventually decided to create an abortion zine, *Our Truths/Nuestras Verdades*, to reflect women's experiences; the publication launched in print and on the web in July 2005, and is currently a project of Exhale. (I'm on the advisory council of Exhale and on the editorial board of *Our Truths/Nuestras Verdades*.)

Projects like Barcklow's, which focus on mining women's experience rather than repeating stale aphorisms, are popping up all around the country. Sarah Varney, a young reporter for NPR, created radio documentaries in which older women tell their pre-*Roe* abortion stories. Varney also produced a series of events called the *Beta Project* to use the stories to help people talk about and better understand abortion. Two other filmmakers, Faith Pennick and Penny Lane, have completed related documentaries. While Lane's *Abortion Diaries* focuses on a diverse spectrum of women aged nineteen to fifty-four, Pennick's is called *Silent Choices* and specifically explores the experiences of black women.

These women are trying to create the kind of activism needed for a legal right that, while constantly under attack, has so transformed society that it is now disingenuous to speculate that women would "go back" if *Roe* were overturned. "Even illegal abortion would look very different today than it did four decades ago," Caitlin Flanagan wrote in a 2007 *Atlantic Monthly* essay, "The Sanguine Sex." "However bad the toll on women's health would be (and it would be very bad), it would be nothing like the carnage of the past. The age of ignorance is gone, and abortion is a simple procedure."

Flanagan is in her fifties and unafraid of offending people—something often attributed not just to her wit, but to her privilege as a wealthy and educated woman. Perhaps younger women, in their own entitlement, will begin to make blasphemous statements even more loudly. The most profane is this: *Why are feminists so obsessed with abortion?* Some of the lingering fascination is due to what the Gloria Steinems of the world might argue—we focus on this right because it is fundamental; having the right to control our bodies is directly associated with the right to control our lives. But I think feminists return to this issue, too, because it was once such a litmus test: *Are you with us or against us?* The abortion decision once appeared to be black-and-white—if you cared about women, then abortion was beyond ethical. Women were right to claim that their lives didn't have to be sacrificed to a mistake made one night in the back of a car. Discussing the value of the fetus or entertaining grief was not the most urgent issue when women were still struggling for basic rights.

Society has changed so much since January 22, 1973, much of it a function of women's liberation movements. Naturally, this also changes the scope of reproductive rights. Many veterans in the pro-choice world have a list of critical issues that the pro-choice movement as a whole tends to avoid. Charlotte Taft likens the terrain in which we now live to a picnic—and a picnic has crumbs that the "ants," or "antis" (political opponents), will pick up. "Part of my definition of a crumb is that it is an issue or question that unavoidably accompanies abortion—that any reasonable person knows is important," Taft wrote in a 2005 essay distributed to abortion providers, "but that we largely greet with silence as a movement . . . When I say these are crumbs I mean that they are issues to which our primary reaction (notice I didn't say response) has been political wrangling, defensiveness, and litigation." Taft lists several of these crumbs: teens and pregnancy, men's involvement in pregnancy and abortion, fetal pain, multiple abortions, poor-quality abortion providers, women who regret having an abortion, late-term abortion, selective abortion for multiple pregnancies, and religion and abortion.

Along these lines, I had my own moment of truth during my fifth month of pregnancy in May 2004. A small moment, but it changed me. I was speaking to a group from Barnard College's Students for Choice when I referred to that object in one's uterus when one is pregnant as a "baby."

A nurse practitioner who was speaking after me interrupted: "*Fetus*, you mean. You said *baby*, but it's a fetus."

"Oh, right," I stammered, blushing. "Oops." I felt foolish, caught in an ignorant mistake. Later, though, I realized that I had always thought of my pregnancy as carrying a baby—that was the word I wanted to use—and I was forcing myself to say "fetus" out of fear. If I said "baby," that meant I wasn't pro-choice, or with the program, or knowledgeable. I thought of other phrases that I forced myself to use too, like "so-called partial-birth abortion" and "antichoice." These phrases suddenly struck me as legal jargon, words in the service of arguments that weren't themselves always meaningful.

Suppressing language, policing ourselves so we don't slip up and say "baby," contributes to a split between our politics and our lives. The personal is political, and any feminist worth her speculum knows that divisions between the two will drain her of strength and dignity.

Is the pro-choice movement ready to change? There is ample evidence that Exhale's once perplexing mission has paid off. To wit, when Senator Hillary Clinton addressed 1,000 abortion rights supporters on the thirty-second anniversary of *Roe v. Wade* in 2005, she asserted her belief in the Supreme Court decision but also admitted that abortion can be "tragic" for some women. Her words sent shock waves through the major pro-choice organizations and spurred the *New York Times* to surmise that the senator was "recalibrating" her position on abortion in preparation for her 2008 bid for the White House. But a mere three years later, on the thirty-fifth anniversary of *Roe*, NARAL President Nancy Keenan confessed that "our community tends to run away every time somebody talks about the many emotions that come with this choice" and "we have not done enough to make people who are 'pro-choice but struggling' feel like they are part of this community."

Exhale has now surpassed the call volume of the Bay Area rape crisis and domestic violence hotlines and their materials are available at hundreds of clinics around the country. They have more providers turning to them to be trained in after-abortion emotional resources than they can service. The desire to help women and do the right thing has always guided the clinic environment, but now there are more ways to provide help—and consciousness has been raised to redirect the focus of clinic workers from countering protesters back to listening to women.

In March of 2007, Aspen Baker was invited onto Fox News, the nation's most conservative major network, to discuss her work at Exhale. People warned her not to do the interview, but Baker wanted to celebrate the fact that Exhale was sending out 2,500 e-cards every month. Martha MacCallum, the host of the show, began the segment by saying to the camera, "Most women probably know somebody who has been through this experience, but have you ever thought of sending them a card?" Without saying a word, Baker felt like her philosophy had already penetrated. If a representative of Fox News would blithely say that we all know someone who has had an abortion—no recrimination, acknowledging the common secret—then it was clear pro-voice activists were breaking through the stalemate around abortion.

"We're modeling respect and listening around this issue," says Baker, "and people are desperate for it."

Is listening enough? Probably not, but it is a crucial move forward.

CHAPTER 4

CAN YOU BE A FEMINIST AND PRO-LIFE?

In 1993, Amy Richards (then the twenty-three-year-old cofounder of the Third Wave Foundation) was on a panel at a local New York City high school discussing feminism, when a sixteen-year-old girl timidly inquired whether one could be pro-life and a feminist. Amy answered promptly: "No. Next question." Amy recalls that Angel Williams, another activist on the panel, looked the girl in the eyes and said, "Being pro-life doesn't make you ineligible to be a feminist." Amy was infuriated by Angel's comment. "The only thing that made me feel better," recalls Amy, "was knowing that I was simply the better feminist, while Angel was willing to compromise feminism's core values."

Years later, after Amy and I had cowritten two books addressing third-wave feminism, we became intrigued by that same recurring question. At a certain point in nearly every college classroom we visited, an earnest woman would raise her hand and recount the ways in which she felt she was a feminist ("I directed my campus production of *The Vagina Monologues*"; "I founded a group in high school to build schools for girls in Afghanistan"; etc.). Then she'd say, "But can you be a feminist and pro-life?"

It's a challenge to combine those identities, but Amy and I have both learned that these women are not asking if bombing an abortion clinic can fall within the realm of feminism. They aren't even wondering if it is okay to keep others from accessing an abortion and still call themselves feminists. They are usually asking if it's okay not to prioritize abortion, not to go to the March for Women's Lives, not to raise money for women's procedures. They are asking if they can believe that abortion is the taking of a life, even a sacred human life, and still be a feminist. If not, then these women (and men) see no alternative than to join the swelling ranks of "I'm not a feminist but . . ." They can't suddenly abandon their belief about fetal life. So, are there organizations that represent the pro-life person who doesn't believe that women are second-class citizens?

There are at least two very visible groups that identify as both pro-woman and pro-life: Democrats for Life of America and Feminists for Life of America. Democrats for Life was founded in 1999, initially with four chapters but has grown to more than forty. While their executive director Kristen Day cites a December 2003 Zogby poll finding that forty-three percent of Democrats oppose abortion except in the case of rape or incest or to save the life of the mother, she also concedes that most Democrats do not want to recriminalize the procedure. While Democrats for Life's leaders in Congress include Jim Oberstar, who helped craft the extremely punitive Hyde Amendment, the stated mission of the group is to make good on the party plank holding that abortion should be rare. In 2005, Democrats for Life began pushing "95-10," a plan they hoped would reduce abortions by ninety-five percent in ten years. The strategy, however, doesn't have a serious plan of action. Their platform doesn't advocate birth control and provides little to inspire a person who wants to be true to both their feminism and the value they place on fetal life.

At first glance, Feminists for Life appears to provide a good haven for the pro-life feminist, but their practices echo that of Democrats for Life. They focus on dismantling abortion without bringing about the pro-woman changes—in particular, access to family planning—that might make abortion less common. (They say that "pre-conception issues" are outside of their mission.) They claim that early feminists were in fact pro-life, but have taken the women's comments so out of context that many historians disagree with their conclusions. Certainly it is true that first-wave feminists such as Elizabeth Cady Stanton and Susan B. Anthony took up the cause of women like

Hester Vaughn, a teenage immigrant in Philadelphia who was condemned to be hanged after she was forcibly impregnated by her employer, cast out on the street, and found with her baby dead—a series of tragedies then judged an infanticide. Anthony and Stanton organized women to protest—arguing that Vaughn was a "victim of a social system that forced women, especially poor women, to murder their illegitimate children or face social ostracism," as Ellen Carol DuBois writes in her 1999 book, *Feminism & Suffrage*. But their critique of Vaughn's treatment cannot be conflated with the message that women should never choose or desire to end an unplanned pregnancy.

Feminists for Life's position that "women deserve better" than the degradation they often face, though, has value. And it is true that if women were more empowered—free of abusive partners, less poisoned by misogyny, had adequate access to health care and education about sex and their bodies—abortion would occur far less frequently. (But the *need* for abortion will never be totally eradicated, according to the late health activist Barbara Seaman, unless society commits to giving vasectomies to all boys after freezing their sperm, and only allowing procreation through *in vitro* fertilization after demonstrating sufficient income and maturity to support a child for eighteen years. No one has jumped on this policy proposal for an abortion-free world.) The sentiments put forth by Democrats for Life and Feminists for Life work well as an ideal—women deserve better than to be left holding the bag for a mutual sexual encounter—but they don't appear to address the fact that people will always have sex.

It's a stultifying myth of feminism that prioritizing abortion rights is the most significant test of your commitment to women. You don't have to go to that march on Washington, you don't have to counsel your friends to have abortions, and you don't have to believe that abortion might be a good option for you. But that is just what you don't have to do. You *do* have to do something to animate your value system. What does it mean to be authentically pro-life and a feminist? Given how reproductive decisions occur within a social framework of so many other personal values, such as one's religion or family culture or self-image, it might seem difficult to actually lay out pro-life strategies that are genuine and don't conflict with women's freedom. None-theless, these parameters strike me as fitting the bill:

Work to make sure women who want to raise their kids have the support to do so: Traditionally, women have taken on the everyday hard work of cultivating the future. In other words, we raise the children. The "future," meanwhile, has it tough. Our often inadequate, frequently cruel foster care system can't handle the more than 300,000 kids thrust into its rigid arms each year, and the "end of welfare" ushered in during Bill Clinton's presidency means that living in poverty is just a part of growing up for thirteen million children in the United States. Yet more and more young women—child-free and mothers, single and partnered—are dealing with the collapse of the nuclear family. Feminists for Life is good at pointing out the ways that some pro-choice organizing, particularly on college campuses, can be downright hostile to early parenting. Sadly, though, they don't raise money to provide the resources they are so mad do not exist. Some of those resources might include: recruiting foster parents; providing family court advo-cates; establishing funds to offer support to low-income or otherwise stressed parents (from formula and diapers to lactation consultants); organizing free emergency babysitting services at trustworthy public locations (like universities) and publicizing them at churches, welfare agencies, and grocery stores.

Loretta Ross has long worked to bridge the divide between women who get abortions—often lower-income and disproportionately black—and abortion rights advocates, who are often middle class and white. "If you're in the field, you know that black women are twelve percent of the female population but get twenty-five percent of the abortions in the country," says Ross, the fifty-five-year-old coauthor of *Undivided Rights: Women of Color Organize for Reproductive Justice* (South End Press, 2004). "Yet black women are saying this is not their issue. I have to ask why not." Ross is national coordinator of SisterSong: Women of Color Reproductive Health Collective, an organization that was instrumental in changing the name of the 2004 pro–abortion rights demonstration in Wash-ington from "March for Freedom of Choice" to "March for Women's Lives."

"We couldn't endorse the march unless they recognized the complex issues that women face," explains Ross. "Every woman who is pregnant wonders if she has a bedroom for that child; can she afford to take off the time to raise that child? Why flatten the decisions around abortion to just abortion? When women don't have jobs or health care, where is the choice? There is nothing worse than a woman aborting a baby she wanted because she couldn't support it." Ross notes that black women were the first to resist the pro-choice/pro-life dichotomy. "A very large percentage of [black] women are personally opposed to abortion but are politically pro-choice," adds Ross, who is one of the architects of the reproductive justice framework. "Women of color agree with not giving unborn children more rights than grown women, but even when they're terminating a pregnancy, they call it a baby. This has been going on as long as we have had the debate."

Support birth control and sex education (along with abstinence): Feminists for Life along with other not-so-feminist-friendly pro-life organizations do not support contraception or sex education. A position paper released by the largest right-to-life educational organization—the American Life League— reads, *The practice of contraception is intrinsically evil and lays the groundwork for other evils such as the act of abortion,* and calls for *an absolute trust in God and His will with regard to the gift of children.* Many pro-life activists consider contraception as the first step in a "slippery slope" that leads to abortion, because, that thinking goes, if you can have sex without fear of pregnancy, you will be more likely to have sex outside of the bounds of marriage. It's undeniable that abstinence from sexual intercourse is the best way to avoid getting pregnant. It's also undeniable that much sexual activity occurs in less than ideal, coherent, and consensual circumstances and that most people have sex more often than the few times it took to conceive their children. However, the best way to truly protect women and men and to improve our bodily health and our potential to reproduce is with honest information about sex, honest talk about personal values, and by modeling the behavior we believe to be most healthy. As the statistics about abstinence-only education attest, people are going to have sex whether or not it's sanctioned.

Work toward early abortion: Later abortions are harder on everyone. They are more expensive ($1,000 to $2,500 or more for a twenty-week procedure, compared to $400 or less for an eight-week procedure) and require greater medical expertise (not to mention up to three days of doctor's visits to complete) and travel expense, as there are very few doctors who do later procedures. They're harder on women (financially and physically) and possibly harder on the fetus (there is contradictory evidence in recent research on fetal pain). A strong abortion rights movement has already meant that women are getting procedures earlier, when the surgery is easier and safer. In 1973, only thirty-eight percent of abortions were performed within the first two months of pregnancy. Today the figure is more than fifty-five percent. Coincidentally, earlier abortions are less controversial among the pro-choice advocates who favor some restrictions (a surprisingly high number of people). It is part of the future of abortion to promote earlier procedures, when the cost is reduced in every way—on the medical system, on the woman, on the fetus, and even in the field of public opinion. "You can't have choice without knowledge," says Merle Hoffman. "And sometimes that knowledge is hard to bear." But given the myriad of factors that might impact one's decision, it is crucial to be frank and fearless about what we know and don't know about the fetus and let women decide for themselves.

Support EC and medical abortion: To encourage earlier abortions, we need to make mifepristone and emergency contraception more readily available, as well as rethink our restrictions on abortion generally. Researchers James Trussell and Felicia Stewart concluded that if emergency contraception (pills that can be taken within ninety-six hours of unprotected sex) were effectively promoted and distributed, they could address an estimated two million unintended pregnancies per year. If their assessment is correct, this initiative would save billions of dollars each year. A study commissioned by New York State comptroller in

2003 (and revised for 2005), entitled "Emergency Contraception: Fewer Unintended Pregnancies and Lower Health Care Costs," estimates "that widely available and easily accessible emergency contraception could result in $233.1 million in savings" for New York State alone, "reducing the 104,776 unintended pregnancies associated with Medicaid-eligible women" by half.

Work against restrictions: For years I have supported the New York Abortion Access Fund, which funded many later-term procedures since women travel to New York City for abortions up to twenty-four weeks. (New York is one of the few places with doctors trained to perform those procedures and a public that supports those doctors—or at least isn't openly hostile.) When doing intake, we would learn why the individual patient was seeking a later procedure, and almost without exception it had to do with restrictions on abortion. These laws became infuriating to me because they didn't make women change their minds about needing a procedure, they merely punished them, making them jump through demeaning hoops at a time when they needed support. Because of the Hyde Amendment, women on public assistance in some states couldn't get a Medicaid-covered procedure; raising money meant waiting to get the abortion. Ditto, parental consent rules. As girls drum up the courage to tell their parents, the pregnancy develops further. According to Susan Cohen, the director of government affairs at the Guttmacher Institute, evidence from around the world shows that placing restrictions on abortion makes it less safe rather than more rare. "In the United States, abortion opponents take credit for the mounting state and federal restrictions on abortion," says Cohen, "rather than working to reduce unintended pregnancy to begin with."

Actively condemn violence: Ani DiFranco's wrenching song "Hello Birmingham" is a letter to that city from her hometown of Buffalo, New York. In 1998, Eric Rudolph bombed New Woman All Women Health Care in Birmingham, Alabama, killing a young off-duty police officer named Robert Sanderson and horrifically maiming clinic nurse Emily Lyons. That same year, a Buffalo doctor named Barnett Slepian who provided abortions was murdered in his home, in front of his children. The bravery that is sometimes required for clinic workers just to show up for their jobs is heartbreaking. And the violence is utterly in conflict with any authentic reverence for life. Feminists for Life offered a reward for any information that could lead to the arrest and conviction of the Birmingham bomber, demonstrating that their pro-life worldview can work in concert with feminist goals.

Truly understand adoption, and work to make sure the birth mother has a voice: When Norma McCorvey's autobiography, *I Am Roe,* was published in 1994, it was dedicated to *"All of the Jane Does who died for Choice."* Yet by the very next year, she had become one of the best-known antiabortion activists in history, joining Operation Rescue. She even petitioned the Supreme Court (unsuccessfully) to have *Roe* overturned. And yet, Norma McCorvey, who never actually had an abortion, nonetheless represents a very silenced, often-mistreated demographic: birth mothers.

Just before Christmas of 2006, I attended an event at which adoption scholar Ann Fessler played the audio pastiche of her interviews with birth mothers who surrendered their children in the years before *Roe.* I perched on the arm of a couch in a Park Avenue apartment and sobbed. I cried for the many women who were conned into relinquishing their children and fed a nonstop barrage of insults, from "You'd be a terrible mother" to "You've brought shame on the family" to "Just pretend this never happened." I cried remembering how intense it was to be pregnant and to give birth—how hormones and pain and extreme physical duress combined into what felt like a near-death experience. I recalled how I really understood—in my loosened pelvis, my stretched-out ribs, and the kicks to my cervix from tiny limbs—the sensitive factory that is our bodies, arduously creating another human. The thought of going through that and being told it didn't matter—*You don't know this baby anyway*—struck me as unbearably cruel. My tears also reflected the poignancy of growing up in a different era, one in which my unplanned pregnancy and subsequent out-of-wedlock parenting can be celebrated and supported, with two sets of parents thrilled to become grandparents. I read Fessler's wonderful book, *The Girls Who Went Away,* and was overwhelmed by the emotional pain the women endured. It's not a fair comparison, perhaps, but I found the stories of women who surrendered their babies just as traumatic and heartbreaking as the stories I've heard of women who had abortions pre-*Roe.*

I spoke with Ann Fessler about adoption. Even if the terrain has shifted radically from the social pressures on girls raised in the 1950s, it's clear that the voice of the birth mother is still very suppressed. "Many [birth mothers] are promised one thing and enter into the misunderstanding that they are committing to a situation with certain protections that, in fact, aren't guaranteed," Fessler says. In many places, for instance, if the mother leaves the state in which the adoption occurred, the contract is broken and she no longer has the right to see her child. "Over the years, all of the laws have gone the way of supporting adoption agencies' needs," she explains. "In some states, women are asked to sign within twenty-four hours of birth, and it is irrevocable." There is less and less of a space for the birth mother to process the experience of having had a baby at all.

"I'm an adoptee, and I'm not dispassionate to the emotional stress that the adoptive parent is feeling," Fessler reveals. "The bottom line, though, is that it is not their child *yet,* and even though this is emotional, the birth mother needs a reasonable amount of time to come to grips with this decision."

Ethical adoption is one piece of a pie that includes foster care, a social safety net that supports struggling families, and a commitment to helping parents raise healthy children. Pro-choice organizations such as Backline in Portland, Oregon are opening up space to discuss adoption in all of its facets. No doubt the room created by these activists and parents will shepherd in new understanding of how to support the adoption option that is so glibly proffered by some politicians.

So, can you be a feminist and pro-life? The answer is a resounding "yes." In fact, finding more and better ways to do just that would be, in a word, revolutionary.

LIBERTY ALDRICH & JOE SAUNDERS WITH THEIR SONS

CHAPTER 5
YOUR MOTHER, SISTER, DAUGHTER, BEST FRIEND: PORTRAITS AND STORIES OF WOMEN WHO'VE HAD ABORTIONS

A few days after the *I had an abortion* T-shirt controversy sprung into gear, amid the daily barrage of phone calls from reporters and talk radio producers, I received a message from a thoughtful young woman named Tara Todras-Whitehill. She worked as a red-carpet photographer for celebrity papparazzo Patrick McMullan, but had amassed quite a body of personal work that reflected her interest in women's lives. Tara, whose mother had had an abortion and was always open with her about it, saw the shirts on CNN. She wanted to photograph women wearing them, and thought she'd start by doing portraits of the women in the film I had made with Gillian.

Of the thirty or so photo shoots we did, perhaps the portrait of Liberty Aldrich with her husband Joe and her sons on the previous page most poignantly reflects on the false divide in the public consciousness between abortion and family. In fact, most women who have abortions do so in the context of being a mother, and often while being a wife or partner too. Liberty struck a chord, also, because hers is perhaps the ideal abortion story—she was educated about her body and her options, had support from friends and family, and had insurance that would pay for the procedure. And the more I heard other people's stories, the more Liberty's struck me as unique—feminists' best efforts to make her experience the norm notwithstanding.

I want every woman who has had an abortion to be as free as possible from guilt and shame about her life experiences. At the same time, I also want to honor the truth of abortion for most women—these are diverse experiences, but often loaded with pain and stress, both internally and externally generated. The personal statements that accompany the portraits in the following pages capture a wide range of reasons why women choose abortion. Often it was in part financial—as in the case of Loretta Ross and Florence Rice, who were already young single mothers when they got pregnant a second time. With many of the women, they were simply too young and not at all prepared to be a mother at that point and under those circumstances. With others, giving birth to a baby seemed to preclude an investment in their own lives; it would have meant saying goodbye to a fellowship, to a career of their choosing, or being forced to stay in a relationship they didn't want with the baby's father. Abortion most heavily impacts the poor and young, and while many of the women in these portraits are now older and financially stable, their lives were decidedly more chaotic when they found out they were pregnant.

Tara's portraits show women who have had abortions as they truly are: mothers, grandmas, friends, career women, lesbians, activists, extroverted, shy, young, old, thoughtful, happy, married, single, and so much more than a statistic.

FLORENCE RICE, BORN MARCH 22, 1919

My mother came from the West Indies and I don't know what happened between her and my father, but she was left with many children to take care of and she just couldn't do it alone . . .

so I grew up in an orphanage and foster care in Harlem. I never saw my mother except once during the entire time that I was growing up. I never got a Christmas card, nothing. When my mother finally came and got me out of the orphanage, I was very angry with her. I became a runaway. I wasn't a very nice child.

Soon, I found myself out in the world by myself and pregnant from a person that I thought loved me—one of those stupid things that young women think. I knew society was not too nice to people who had babies and no marriage. I heard about people who just did abortions, too, there was no secret. At that time, I did not know it was illegal, because abortion was something people discussed and talked about. I'll always remember Lenox Avenue and 117th Street, where I threw the box [of pills that could cause a miscarriage] away because, somehow, I didn't want to get rid of her. I just wanted something to love; I think that's probably what it was. I was sixteen when I had my daughter. They put her in my arms and she looked at me like, *If you don't want me, then I don't want you either!* You know, she just had that look—and I fell in love with her then. I began to dream about giving her the opportunities that I never had.

So I went to work in a laundry. My salary was $12.41 a week—it was the 1930s. I worked and I took care of her. Later on, I sort of went with someone else and found myself pregnant again—but I knew I wasn't going to have any more babies. I was *not* going to be like my mother. It was just as simple as that.

I can remember where I went for the abortion very well. I just walked there in Harlem, and the woman was ready for me. It was a midwife, a woman—she was very receptive, very warm. She did what needed to be done, I paid her, and I left. I can't recall that it was painful, but I guess it probably was. I just felt lucky to be able to get the money to even do it. I did get an infection and I ended up in Harlem Hospital, where the nurses were very nasty because they wanted to know who did it. These nurses said to me, "Oh, well, then you are going to die in this bed [of the infection]." I was scared but I was not going to tell them who did it because it was none of their business. But no one could tell me what I should have done and what I shouldn't. I did what *I* thought was important for me to be able to continue with my life. I have no regrets.[*]

---

[*]From an interview conducted by Gillian Aldrich in 2004 for the film *I Had an Abortion*. All interviews were conducted by Jennifer Baumgardner unless otherwise indicated.

GLORIA STEINEM, BORN MARCH 25, 1934

I grew up with no discussion of sexuality. I think the most information I got was from a little pamphlet that Kotex used to put out—and it was all about menstruation . . .

When I was in high school, the greatest shame was to get pregnant. It was the worst thing that could happen to you. It was most likely to get you banished from your family, disapproved of by your neighborhood, turned into somebody who was clearly not a "nice girl." And in my neighborhood growing up—a very working-class, factory-working neighborhood in Toledo—there were clearly only two types of girls: nice and not nice. There was also very little knowledge about reliable contraception, so most of the people who I knew got married either before they graduated from high school or immediately afterwards—and most of them got married, at least in part, because they had to.

As a senior in college, I was engaged to a wonderful man, but not somebody I should have married. That would have been a disaster for both of us. So I broke off the engagement with him and that was part of my motivation for taking a fellowship and going to India. He and I were together again just before I left, and soon I kind of knew—or feared—that I was pregnant. I was living in London, waiting for my visa to India which took a very long time, working as a waitress with no money, no friends, dark winter days, trying to figure out what to do.

You know, in a way, ambivalence about abortion is a function of its legality. I was not ambivalent. I was desperate. I did not see any way that I could possibly give birth to someone else and also give birth to myself. It was just impossible. So there was not one moment, not one millisecond, of me thinking it would be a good idea to have a child.

In London at that time [the mid-1950s], if you got two physicians to say that having a child would endanger your health or your mental health, then it was possible to get a legal abortion—not easy, but it was possible. After many weeks of fear, confusion, and magical thinking that I would somehow have a miscarriage, I found this wonderful doctor who had many writers and poets as his patients, and he said, "All right, I'll help you. But you must promise me two things. You must never tell anyone my name and you must promise me to do what you want with your life."

So he signed what was necessary and sent me to a woman surgeon, who gave me an anesthetic, so I was not conscious for the actual procedure. Afterwards, she gave me pills and told me to be aware of the amount of bleeding, but it wasn't much. So I just went home and stayed in bed for the weekend and went back to work as a waitress—but with such a feeling of lightness and freedom and gratitude.

I thought everybody was supposed to feel guilty, so I used to sit and think and think and think; but I could not make myself feel guilty for even a moment. Far from feeling guilty, it was the first time I had taken responsibility for my own life. It was the first time I hadn't been passive. That I had said, *No, I'll take responsibility for my own life, I am going to make a decision.* And you know, to this day, I would raise flags on all public buildings to celebrate the chance I had to make that decision.

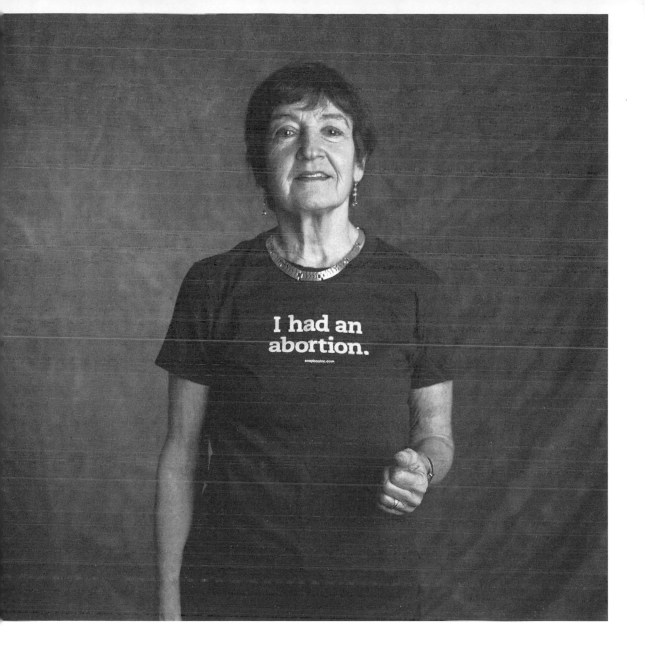

SALLY ALDRICH, BORN JULY 6, 1940

*I grew up in the late '50s, and there was really very little birth
control. The birth control pill had not been invented. When I
went off to college, I was determined to remain a virgin . . .*

In fact, I remember saying to my mother, *I want to be just like my older sister. I am going to get an apartment in New York. I am going to get a super job in New York. I am going to go to Europe. And I am going to be married a virgin.* I dated. I teased boys. I necked with my boyfriends, but I was terrified of real sex. I was terrified of becoming pregnant. In fact, one of my best friends in high school got pregnant our senior year and had to drop out. It was a stigma that you did not want attached to yourself.

So my answer to life was to not have sex with anybody . . . until I finally did at age twenty-two for the first time. No protection. To my horror, I got pregnant. You occasionally heard stories about somebody who had tried to have an abortion using a coat hanger and how frightening an experience that was. I knew that I had to face having an abortion, and just accepting the reality that this is what had happened to me was very hard.

I had a girlfriend who was very sophisticated, and I went to her and told her I was pregnant. And she set me with this doctor. All I remember was that he said he would scrape my uterus, and that would cause [the pregnancy] to eventually dislodge, and that I would pass it. It wasn't really painful. There wasn't a nurse there, because I remember when I first went to the office, he was taking me between patients, and he was on the phone. And I remember getting off the table, and him grabbing me by my arm and making a pass at me, and me just pushing myself away and being totally revolted.

My boss, Keith, was very sympathetic with me during all of this. I told him that I'd had an abortion. Now that I was no longer a virgin, he felt that I was safe to date. I started dating Keith that summer, and by November he proposed to me. We were making wedding plans, and I had this diaphragm, and it was kind of awkward for me to use. He got impatient with me that I wasn't spontaneous enough. So, guess what, I got pregnant a second time.

That was even more horrifying to me—that *that* could happen to me twice. And I just knew that going into marriage pregnant, I would not have a chance. I'd seen my sisters who were much older than me coming home as newlyweds with babies, and being hectic, and I just didn't want to start a marriage that way.

I called my girlfriend and she set me up with this doctor up in Harlem. I went by myself in a taxi. He was very kindly and he put me under. I remember that he was in a green hospital gown and I was in a green hospital gown—[it was] very above-board. When I woke up, I just cried and cried from this tremendous feeling of relief.

Not long after I married Keith, a woman knocked at my door and asked me if I'm Sally Aldrich. I said yes. She asked me if I needed a housecleaner. I said, "Well, thank you, but I really don't. I do it myself." So then, it's about a month later, the doorbell rings. I'm about to go to work, I have my red coat on, and I'm handed a subpoena right at my door. I have to appear at the grand jury that day. The only thing I could think of was that this doctor is being investigated for abortion. And at first I thought, *Oh my God! My face is going to be all over the* Daily News, *and my father's going to be commuting on the Chappaqua train, and there I'll be!*

So I take a taxi to go downtown, and I'm in a police investigation room. These are the days before Miranda rights—we're talking about very early spring 1964—so no one has led me to believe that I have any rights at all. This one policewoman looked at me and said, "Do I look familiar to you?" I looked at her and I said, "Yes. You asked me for a job as a housecleaner." She said, "We were tailing your doctor. He's committed many abortions, a huge crime. And you have committed a crime also."

So I'm twenty-three and it looks like I'm going to have to go to jail. It seemed my life would be ruined because I had an abortion. I have no idea how many women were actually hauled in that day. I know there were a lot. But this doctor was somebody who was a practicing gynecologist at Harlem Hospital, who obviously was seeing totally different kinds of people. Some black, some white, young women, older women, women in this plight, and he obviously was doing something for them—and he was not charging a lot. All of us, when we realized that there were others in the same boat, began to talk to each other. We began to share stories. For the first time that day I felt like a normal person. That I wasn't just a criminal, and in fact, that there were other women who had gone through the same experience I had gone through. It gave me a feeling of strength before I went into that courtroom. When I got into the grand jury itself, they were really trying to intimidate me and I had this red coat on, and I felt like I had this large scarlet A on me. I realized they were trying to make this very sexual.

"Were you wearing clothes?" they asked. I started to say I was wearing a hospital gown and I was cut off: "Just answer the question!" At a certain point, my shame turned to indignation, and I had this feeling of pride about being the scarlet letter. And I managed to say without being cut off that I really felt that this doctor was a great hero and that he helped many women.

Afterwards, it did seem odd to have done this huge thing and not to have anyone to talk to about it. My mother lived out in the suburbs in Chappaqua and I was living in Manhattan. My mother was also an artist, and one day she suggested that we meet at the Guggenheim Museum. I think my seeing her that day was not so much to see artwork. I was going to tell her the story of the abortion with my husband; I didn't want to mention the first one. So we're finally having lunch in the cafeteria. Now, my mother was forty when I was born, so I was a late last child and we were from very different eras. We're eating, and I said, "Mother, there's really something I have to tell you." And she said, "What is that, dear?" I said, "Mother, I've had an abortion." And my mother was eating her yogurt and she said, "Well, dear, I've had two. Now let's go look at the paintings."

It was just such a relief that I could tell her—and that she could one-up me—although she didn't know it, but she really equaled my experience. I had always thought of her as such a puritanical person, but I become closer and closer to her after that. I realized there was nothing I couldn't tell my mother after that, which was wonderful.

I never found out what happened to the doctor after I was called to testify that he had given me an abortion. My husband and I assumed that his license was taken away at least for a while, but there was no mention of it in the papers. Pretty soon after the day I was subpoenaed, I began having my children and I didn't really think about it much after that, to be honest. I don't even recall his name at this point.[*]

*From an interview conducted by Gillian Aldrich in 2004.

BARBARA EHRENREICH, BORN AUGUST 26, 1941

I was born in Butte, Montana, and we moved a lot as I was growing up, due mainly to upward mobility. We went from the mines of Butte to the white-collar middle class of Los Angeles . . .

My parents were liberal in the Roosevelt sense, but my mother, who had been raised by her grandparents, sent me very mixed signals about sex. She conveyed on the one hand that prudery was very silly, but also no sex until marriage. She really never said why and, honestly, I never asked. I wasn't sexually active in high school anyway. I was a total nerd and just happy with my books.

In college, at Reed [in Portland, Oregon] my closest friend had to have an illegal abortion. I lent her the money—$400, which was *huge* to us at the time. That was the first I saw of abortion and what it meant that it was illegal. I mean, she went to Seattle where there was a real doctor who helped women and it was safe, but the stealth of it and the worry and the money made a big impression on me. Up until then, I had heard of abortion but thought, *That could never happen to me*. As soon as I helped my friend, I woke up and realized that of course it could.

I have had two abortions—both in the '70s. My abortions were not morally or emotionally wrenching for me. I was just relieved each time when I had the procedure. I already had two young children. I was a freelance writer living in Long Island, separated from my children's father and doing adjunct teaching. I had a hard time putting together enough of an income as it was.

By the time I had the abortions, I was not only a feminist, I was active in the women's health movement, writing the books *For Her Own Good* and *Witches, Midwives, and Nurses*. I was one of those women crusading against unnecessary surgery, calling for less hazardous contraceptives and a more humane approach to childbirth. In that context, I had made my contraceptive choice to use a diaphragm, because although it was not the most effective, it was the safest. Actually, my method was diaphragm with legal abortion as a backup—so abortion was, in fact, part of my contraceptive plan, my birth control. Women do use abortion as backup nowadays, but they often don't acknowledge it. I'm referring to women who get pregnant purposefully, for instance, but assume that legal abortion will be available as a backup should the child they're carrying have Down's syndrome or another abnormality they decide they can't handle.

MARION BANZHAF, BORN SEPTEMBER 12, 1953

*I was raised in Central Florida in a religious home.
I sensed that I was a lesbian at a pretty young age, though I didn't
know consciously what that even was . . .*

If I were to describe my early sexual experiences, I think I wanted to, basically, fuck the dyke part right out of me. I lost my virginity as a camp counselor after graduating high school and then headed off to the University of Florida in Gainesville. At college, immediately I had a new boyfriend, Kevin, and went to get on the pill, but we had already had sex. I started getting really sick in the mornings. It was the beginning of the '70s and all of us girls in the dorm had begun talking—you know, the blind leading the blind—about sex and our bodies. And somebody said, "Oh, wait, morning sickness is a symptom of pregnancy. You didn't get your period, right? You're pregnant." And I was.

Kevin wanted to get married, but I wasn't really in love with him. His view was that we would drop out of school and we would go live with his parents and he would work at the Owens Corning glass factory, where his father worked. And I would stay home with his mother and take care of the baby. This was his plan, and it sends shudders up my spine still to think of it. So I was getting more and more desperate. I thought about killing myself rather than live with Kevin's plan. When I was about ten weeks pregnant, the editor of the *Alligator*, which was the paper of the University of Florida, broke the law and printed abortion-referral information. Abortion was legal then in Hawaii, New York, and California, and there was this group called Clergy Consultation Service, which was a group of ministers who set up referral networks between clinics in New York and other places around the country. The editor was arrested, but I got the newspaper and I immediately called the number. This was heaven-sent. I learned all about what I had to do. I would have to go to New York, and I would need, besides the plane fare to get to New York, $150 for the abortion.

I was sitting around with my girlfriends in my dorm room, and we thought abortion should be legal everywhere, so we put together a petition and I came up with the idea that we should solicit donations for my abortion fund. We went out to the quad on a sunny October day. I would approach people and say, "I'm pregnant, I don't want to be. I've got to get to New York to get an abortion. Will you contribute, and will you sign this petition so that abortion can be legal?" We raised about $350 within a couple of days.

I flew to New York by myself. When I got to the clinic, there were probably about 300 women there. It's like everybody east of the Mississippi came to New York for their abortions. And so I went in and I got on the table, and the doctor said, "You're just on the borderline, I might not be able to do this." I begged and pleaded, and I told him I would go kill myself on the streets of New York City if he didn't do it. So he did. When he learned I was from Florida, he asked me where my bikini tan line was.

This was really an abortion mill, frankly. It took all of about five minutes. Five, ten minutes max—vacuum aspiration. And then get up and walk yourself to the recovery room, where you sat for twenty minutes and then they cut you loose, and then there was the next woman in the room right behind you.

Afterwards, I was thrilled. I was so happy. I was so relieved. It didn't hurt. Even the cramp didn't matter. I was so happy to see that blood. I felt like my life was beginning over again. And I didn't really have time to look around, but I was skipping down the street—and the great thing about New York is that I could skip down the street—and I was singing. And nobody cared because it was New York. I remember I saw a little baby in a carriage and a mom and I thought, *Oh, I'm so glad that's not me*. It was just overwhelming relief that I could go on with my life again.

Thinking back on it, I developed a different sense of confidence after that abortion experience. I felt like I had control over what I was going to do with the rest of my life.*

---

*Some of this is derived from an interview conducted by Gillian Aldrich in 2004. Several additions were made from interviews I subsequently conducted in 2006 and 2007.

LORETTA ROSS, BORN AUGUST 16, 1953

My introduction to sexuality was a kidnapping and a rape.
I was eleven years old at the time, with my Girl Scout troop at
an amusement park . . .

I got separated from my troop and as I'm wandering around this amusement park, a guy offered me a ride home. Next thing I knew, I was taken into some woods and raped. Fortunately for me, if there is a good side to it, he actually delivered me back to my neighborhood so I could get home. I remember very clearly that I had on white jeans. They were covered in blood. My mother took one look at me and said, "Oh, you've started your period." And as I was trying to explain to her what happened, she started berating me for not being with the rest of the troop!

So I didn't tell my mother about the rape until three years later, and what caused me to tell her about it was that I had an older cousin who used to babysit me quite a bit and he initiated sexual activity with me. He was twenty-seven; I was fourteen. When I became pregnant from that, I had to explain to my mother my whole sexual career, such as it was—one rape and then incest. She actually started beating me for being pregnant. I remember how painful that was—not the beating, but the fact that I was being punished for being pregnant as a result of incest.

Because my mother was raised by her grandmother who had been a slave, we had these strong Victorian values that dominated our house. For instance, my mother's idea of undergarments was like five different things—I mean, the bra and the panties were the least of what she thought you should put under your clothes. This was 1968, 1969, so we actually explored the option of me getting an underground abortion because we lived in Texas, so close to Mexico. A lot of girls went across the border to get abortions, but a lot of them didn't come back. Given my options, I had the baby.

I had a scholarship to Radcliffe at the time and that was such a big honor because we were the first generation to go to college and all that. But after I had the baby, they withdrew the offer. They said I wasn't the right moral character for them. I got a scholarship to go to Howard University, which is how I ended up living in Washington, D.C. I was a different kind of freshman, because I was a parent. When you are a teen mother, childhood gets left behind. Even though I had had a baby, my mother refused to sign the permission form for me to get birth control. So, predictably, at college I became pregnant again. Like most teenagers, I was in a fog.

D.C. was one of those rare places that legalized abortion before *Roe*, so I was able to have a safe, legal hospital abortion. But I still needed my mother's consent. She saw the pregnancy as punishment—maybe a punishment from God, but at the very least, she saw it as a punishment for breaking her rules. She was not going to give me permission. Meanwhile, I was not one to romanticize teen pregnancy since I already had a one-year-old. I was very clear that this child I already had will have no future if I mess around and have a brother or a sister for him. I was so crystal clear. I never waivered. It was a challenge to graduate from high school with a baby that woke up at four in the morning needing a feeding. I didn't see anything romantic or cute or inevitable about being the mother of more than one kid at my age. I ended up forging her signature on the consent form and, consequently, having a very late-term abortion because of all that I had to go through to get the consent and get the money.

I don't even know if they do the saline procedure anymore. It's where they take a scarily long needle and insert it in your stomach and shoot in some fluid that actually ends up killing the fetus. It also induces labor so that, well, it's like having a baby, only it's an aborted fetus. The abortion was painful. It was scary. It is by no means a decision anybody makes lightly.*

---

*From an interview conducted by Gillian Aldrich in 2004.

JACKIE WOS, BORN FEBRUARY 18, 1958
(WITH FABIA CLOSSON, BORN OCTOBER 5, 1962)

*I was born and raised in Switzerland. My mom came from a
farm, and Dad was an orphan from Colmar, France, who had
been deported during the Second World War to Switzerland . . .*

His mother had been sexual molested by her father and bore her father's kids. My mom became pregnant with my sister when I was eleven and my brother was thirteen. She was surprised to be pregnant so late in life and told us later that she didn't know if she wanted to carry the child.

I had a very strict sexual upbringing. I left home when I was a teenager. I became sexually active when I was fifteen. Before that, I had been molested twice—once by an uncle when I was four or five, and then by a teacher when I was eight years old. Between the ages of twelve and fifteen, I was very anxious to know whether I was a virgin or not. Another teacher of mine seduced me, and I was intrigued, so eventually we made love and I realized that I had been a virgin. I was fifteen.

I always thought women were attractive but I didn't know how to meet women that wanted women, so I just went out with men—that was easier. By the time I was eighteen, I was in bands and I came to New York City and met the guy that became my husband. I was playing my guitar in a club, we dated in Central Park, and then my visa ran out, so he married me. I liked him and lived with him for four years, but it was more of a visa thing. I was in a rock band and my periods had stopped for two or three months, I guess out of stress, so I stopped taking my birth control pills because I thought it was then safe. I passed out in the subway one morning, and when I went to the clinic, I learned that I was six weeks pregnant.

The abortion clinic was in New York, near Central Park, I don't even remember the address, but it was kind of industrial—like women were on a conveyor belt and *next, next,* and *next* it was you. At the door there were some people showing pictures of fetuses and shouting how sinful it was. My husband dragged me away from them. I guess I was a little groggy, so they did not really hurt my feelings too much. I was also messing up my life with drugs at the time.

In 1985, I really fell in love with a guy and lived with him for eight years. He was also an incest survivor, so sex with him was easier than with other people, not so aggressive. I got pregnant in 1989, but he was a drunk and an addict and I knew I couldn't raise a kid with him. I could not trust the guy for anything. I should have ended the relationship, but I loved him and hoped he would stop doing painful things to himself and me. I think I would have loved to have the child, but the idea of being a single mom frightened me. I was too scared to do it on my own. I needed some nurturing, someone telling me it was all right to be pregnant, to help me find some trust within myself. He was incapable of helping me.

I would have loved to have had children, but I never felt like I was with the right guy, and now I am getting too old and I'm sorry for it. I have been with my girlfriend, Fabia, for twelve years, but it doesn't look like we are going to have children. I think about adopting, but I'd need to have more money. I have been a limo driver for the past nine years. I just got into a new company and I am looking forward to doing my best and going to work every day. I'd have to deal with my incest and molestation and the depression that goes with it in order to have kids.

GILLIAN ALDRICH, BORN FEBRUARY 6, 1969

I think I sort of always knew what abortion was,
but the first time I had a conscious experience of it was while I
was visiting my dad, the summer going into ninth grade . . .

My parents were divorced, and my mom was a bit of a hippie while my dad was a born-again Christian. He told me my mother had an abortion before my brother and I were born and definitely allowed me to believe that she had done this awful thing, essentially *killing* a baby. He took no responsibility for it. It totally made me cry. I called my mom and said, "How could you have done that? I could have had this older brother or sister and you killed them . . ." My mom, of course, was furious. She said, "How *dare* your father frame it this way. We both made this decision; if anything, he pushed for it."

By the time I was in high school and starting to think for myself, I decided I was pro-choice. My first year in college, I went down to D.C. for this big pro-choice march. I don't think I was pro-choice because of my mom, although she had by this point shared her two abortion stories with me. It's odd, I could hear about my mom's abortions with an open mind, but I found it embarrassing when she tried to discuss things like sex with me. I didn't suffer from having a strict parent, but just the opposite—she was too *Free to Be . . . You and Me* for my comfort. For instance, once, two guy friends drove me and a friend to my family's vacation spot in Rhode Island. When we got there, the guys wanted to sleep over. My grandmother was very strict and said that they could sleep in the car; *not* in the house. Meanwhile, my mother took me aside and decided it was time to talk to about the pill. I had made it clear that these guys were just friends and I was nowhere *near* having sex, but she didn't seem to accept that, nor did she discuss any limits, or the seriousness of sex—she just offered up birth control.

So I knew about birth control, obviously, but I didn't always take care of myself once I began having sex. I lost my virginity at seventeen, and although I was usually on the pill, I think I felt sort of invincible when it came to pregnancy. At age thirty, I had been dating Pete, who is now my husband, for a little over a year when I was suddenly very nauseous and my boobs got big, and I suspected I was pregnant. I had recently gone off the pill and we were doing the pull-out thing because I was going through a phase where I thought the hormones were bad for me. Now I realize how crazy that was.

Why would you *not* be on the pill? The night I was going to take the test, Pete was very emotional. His father was really sick and his cat had just died, so he was saying things like, "If this is a baby, maybe the universe is trying to tell us something by bringing us new life, and maybe we should do this."

I had zero sentimentality, and didn't want to even open that door. I thought: *If there is a baby in here, it's not staying.* I knew it would destroy our relationship. I thought of him staying in this job he hated, and how miserable he'd be. Neither of us was mature enough. We weren't young, but we had a lot of growing up to do, and a lot of issues to work out: anger, abandonment, alcohol . . . There was no way it would be a good thing. I would end up alone, and not a piece of me felt ready to handle being a mother. We took the test, and although I was sad knowing I'd be having an abortion, there wasn't a flicker of *Should we?*

We went to this New York City clinic. There were protesters in monk clothes holding pictures of fetuses and yelling in my face, but Pete physically shielded me, and I wouldn't look at them. The place was kind of like a factory. The counseling session was a joke. I thought that there would be more of an emotional support system in the clinic itself, but there wasn't. They wanted to show me the sonogram. I was like, *Why do this now?* Then I got into a gown and it was literally twenty sad women just sitting in a room; they would call one woman at a time and the next woman would shuffle off in her gown. It was surreal.

I didn't want anesthesia because it seemed ethically wrong to me to be totally out for it—I felt like I should have to really experience it. But in the procedure room there were suddenly five people in front of me in masks, and the doctor started coming at me with these big instruments and I yelled, "Wait, wait, *wait!!!!* Is this going to hurt? What am I going to feel?" I was so scared, I guess, that the doctor just overrode my decision to have local and knocked me out. Next thing I knew, I was being wheeled into a room that looked like a World War II hospital—a big room with a bunch of women on gurneys. Some were crying, some were sleeping; they were all in their own private world, dealing with whatever it was they were dealing with. Then they gave us juice and a cookie and I just wanted to get out of that morbid shuffling line and be with someone who would comfort me. As soon as I came out and saw Pete, I started bawling. You know how it is when you hurt yourself as a kid and you are fine until you see your mom? That's how I felt.

We got married a couple of years later, and then about five months into married life, right after 9/11, I had this strong urge to start a family. Pete was trying to make records with his band at that point, and wasn't ready to prioritize a 9-to-5 job, so he said, "Just give me a year to see what I can do with my music, and then we'll try."

That Sylvia Ann Hewlett book came out [Creating a Life: Professional Women and the Quest for Children] around then. There was something retrograde about her attitude, but her facts [demonstrating that fertility declines precipitously throughout your thirties] were correct and I think they were making a lot of people feel anxious. I was thirty-three. I kind of messed up my pill around then and Pete said, "If you want to try and get pregnant in six months, why not go off it, let your body get used to it, and if it accidentally happens, then it was meant to be." I immediately became pregnant. When I took the test and I saw that cross, I had about thirty seconds of wanting to jump out the window. I was scared because I knew we were going to do it this time. The first thing I said to Pete was, and this is so dumb, but I said, "I'm sorry, I know you wanted a year." He said, "Are you kidding? This is great!" Then I allowed myself to be excited, and the first person I called was my mom. She had a disappointing response. She was worried that we weren't in a good enough place financially to start a family. I was so clearly celebrating and she was living in some anxiety I didn't share. It stung.

I directed the I Had an Abortion film just after my daughter was born. I had always been ashamed of my mother's abortion story. I saw it as she was selling out this doctor because she testified in front of a grand jury that he had given her an illegal abortion. I wasn't even sure if I should interview her at first, but once I did, I think I forgave my mother for not being a freedom fighter. It made me see her with less judgment. Here was this young girl from the suburbs in 1960; she was wowed by glamorous New York and terrified of her parents' opinion. And, as she pointed out to me, not only was it a time before feminism, but it was a time before Miranda rights. She literally had no idea what her rights were when she was hauled in that day. How could I be disappointed in her for being a human being in that moment, for being scared?

AMY RICHARDS, BORN FEBRUARY 9, 1970

*I have no issues with talking about
having had an abortion . . .*

Many times I have had the experience of mentioning it during a lecture or at a panel or even just at a dinner party, and later had someone come up to me and thank me for being open. I'm not really doing it on purpose, I just have no guilt about having had an abortion, I had no medical problems as a result of it, I liked the doctor, I liked the staff where I had it, the boyfriend who I was dating at the time was totally supportive of me, and my friends at the time supported me too. I didn't have any horror stories of waking up and feeling like I've just been through triage or feeling really alone. I never thought: *Omigosh, what have I done?*

I had an abortion a week after my twentieth birthday: February 15, 1990. My boyfriend at the time was living in Philadelphia and I was living in Oregon, and he came out to be with me when I had the abortion. There was no question that I would keep the pregnancy, but there *was* a question of whether or not I could afford the abortion. It never would have been that I would have had to raise that money from strangers, it was just a matter of how willing I was to call in favors from family and friends. My boyfriend and I together came up with the $200. And that was not a huge issue, but I did have a moment when I was like, *Two hundred dollars?!* That was an airplane ticket! It seemed like an outrageous amount of money at the time.

The only thing that sort of gives me guilt about having an unwanted pregnancy has to do with the fact that I grew up with less financial stability than most of my friends. When I was little, my mother and I struggled and I was self-conscious that all of my friends were so much richer. My mother went on to make more and more money over the years, and finally we lived a middle-class life where I had designer clothes and even went to an Ivy League college. All I ever wanted to be was a middle-class girl. I think that when I got pregnant and had an abortion, I felt dirty. All of these stereotypes that I had fled from throughout my life suddenly came to fruition. It was like, *of course* this would happen to me, because I'm not really a nice middle-class girl. I feared the stereotype of people who have abortions.

Thirteen years later, when I was pregnant with my first son, I found out at the eight-week sonogram that I was actually pregnant with triplets. It was a huge shock to me because I did not use fertility drugs. I did a lot of research about my options and I made the decision to have a selective reduction. That meant that my son, who was a stand-alone fetus at the time, would continue to term and then there were identical twins that were aborted. The doctor punctured the uterus and gave them each a shot of potassium chloride in the heart. It's instant death—I mean, that's essentially what it is. After I went through the procedure, my boyfriend Peter was much more traumatized than I was, even though hospital policy didn't allow him to witness the procedure.

I don't remember feeling sad about my reduction. I was sorry that I had to be in this position, but when I thought of all of my resources, including myself, my body, and what I was trying to preserve—my relationships, my work, my ability to work—I knew that reducing the pregnancy from three to one was making the best decision that I possibly could. I could form remorse and guilt to go along with knowing that decision was the best, but what was remorse going to get me? You know, it's like I'm making this decision, there's nothing I can do about it once I've done it, and so let's move on.

I later wrote about having had this kind of abortion for the *New York Times Sunday Magazine* and was instantly vilified for not being sufficiently devastated by it. I get a lot of e-mail directed to *Amy Richards: Baby Killer*. Selective reductions are only becoming more popular as people continue to use assisted reproductive technologies to get pregnant. I pursued having that essay published because I was attempting to pull the veil back on this procedure, and I was disappointed by the response of many in the "pro-choice" community who thought honesty about my experience "hurt" the cause.

I have an online advice column and frequently speak at colleges. I meet so many girls who are trying to make sense of abortion. They really want to support abortion rights, they feel that they're feminists, they're respectful of choices that somebody else might make, but at the end of the day just can't say, "I'm pro-choice," or, "I support abortion." I feel for those people because

I think the majority of us *are* that person. The fact is that no one, regardless of her politics, knows what she would do when faced with an unwanted pregnancy; you don't know until you are in the moment.[*]

[*]Much of this is derived from an interview conducted by Gillian Aldrich in 2004, though several additions were made from conversations between me and Amy in 2007.

GEORGE MONOS, BORN AUGUST 21, 1970,
AND DENISE OSWALD, BORN APRIL 24, 1970

George: I was born in Astoria, Queens, in 1970. My parents were both from the Midwest. My father's parents came here from Greece, he was a theater director; my mother was Polish and a dental assistant. My father had bad teeth and they met in her chair. They came to New York City in the mid-'60s to let my dad's career take off, but it never did. So they struggled, he drove a cab. We lived in East New York until 1977 when one of our neighbors was killed, so we moved.

My parents never really had much of a relationship romantically. I'd say my father was troubled sexually and my mother was explosive sexually. They divorced when I was ten. I have an older sister by two years. My stepfather moved in on the day my father moved out. [My stepfather] was more of a masculine presence than my dad—he was also an alcoholic. We really butted heads. My mother's attitude once she married my stepdad was: *This is my chance, I wish I didn't have kids. Fuck you, get out.* I was very aware of my mother's sex life—her sexuality was very in-your-face.

I met Denise in 1989 in my first year of college. She was at Hofstra on Long Island. I was at FIT [Fashion Institute of Technology]. She was hot. I was entranced, especially because she was part of a hardcore punk scene—no women or girls were part of that. I was very impressed. We had this immediate attraction and came from a similar background of feeling like we didn't belong in our families. I never felt wanted. Denise was adopted into a volatile family where her older brother dominated. The first time we hung out, we stayed up all night talking. We had a way deeper connection than we were ready to handle at nineteen.

Denise: When I met George, I'd been periodically seeing a guy at Columbia University, a friend of a friend. He wasn't a boyfriend, more of an occasional hookup. Just before George and I got together, this guy and I had unprotected sex. It was not in keeping with me to do that. I lost my virginity at fourteen and was always on the pill and very responsible. I grew up in Yonkers, which is a very working-class city in parts, and saw the misery of teen pregnancies up close. I knew not to have that life.

With George, I felt like I'd met the person I wanted to spend the rest of my life with. A month into our intense romance, I found out I was pregnant from this other guy. I didn't have that kind of relationship where I could talk to my parents. I had to be the good daughter because of my brother's constant crazy behavior. Also, my mother miscarried many times, and had twins that were stillborn. Discussions of pregnancy were very fraught. I felt like I couldn't mislead George—you don't go off and have an abortion and hide it from the person you're involved with—but I was freaked out too, and I really needed to talk to someone I trusted and was connected to, so I talked to him.

It's funny, because at first George was really supportive. I don't re-member you freaking out on me.

George: I think I was trying to play a part . . .

Denise: You took it better than I expected.

George: I was shocked. I was trying to do what I thought you were supposed to do in an after-school-special kind of way, but in fact I wanted to run, which I eventually did. I suddenly judged Denise as someone who was not good enough for me; it was a horrible thing to learn that I was not as open-minded as I once thought and not as good of a person. I think it was a result of growing up in a household of two women and they were both very sexually in-my-face. And I think I saw Denise suddenly as this very sexual being in a way that I wasn't and your "sex" side overtook your common sense and that's how come that happened to you. Suddenly you were like all of the women in my life who were sexual and screwed up that I needed to get away from. So I broke up with you.

Denise: I was devastated. We both knew we had something. I thought we would spend the rest of our lives together. The day of the procedure I was really nervous and anxious. A friend took me for the abortion and I was under for it. When I woke up, I felt this kind of pain I had never experienced before. The *worst,* deepest pain in my ovary area, like the worst cramps of your life, but that doesn't really get at it. It lasted at least twenty-four hours.

George: Years later, after we were both out of college, we ran into each other at a restaurant. I was meeting a mutual friend for dinner who brought Denise without telling me. At first it was sort of awkward. I was terrified. I was with my girlfriend at the time. Denise and I were around each other several times more over the following months through that same mutual friend, and then we hung out a few more times on our own. We developed a great friendship.

Denise: It seemed like we were going to be friends. I offered to cook for his birthday.

George: That night I realized that I was in love with her and that we had a difficult decision to make—whether our relationship should evolve romantically or whether we should remain friends. I valued our friendship so much, and due to its intensity already, we'd be missing the warm-up stages of dating. There's no toe in the pool. It was jump-in-the-deep-end or stay-in-your-chair. After a few months, I boldly said we should buy an apartment together. And we did.

Denise: The abortion will still come up periodically, and with it is a lingering fear I have of George's judgment. Not all the time; not every time it comes up.

George: For me, I think the abortion will stand as a symbol that I thought of myself as this open, loving guy, but I wasn't.

ANI DIFRANCO, BORN SEPTEMBER 23, 1970

The first time I got my period, my mother, a big feminist, wanted to have a party to celebrate it. I was mortified, but I guess the lesson there is that she was really open with me . . .

about what it meant to have a reproductive system—both the harder realities of it and the glory.

When I was fifteen, I had a thirty-year-old boyfriend. My mother encouraged me to get on birth control. I went to Planned Parenthood in Buffalo, New York, and said, "Um, I'm a virgin and I want to have sex. Can I get birth control?" The women at the clinic literally paraded me around. "This is *Annie*,"—"*Ah*-nee," I'd say—"And *Annie* is getting birth control before she has sex for the first time!" They were so impressed that I was planning it all out before I did anything. A few years later, though, I began thinking that taking hormone pills was not what I wanted. I went off of the pill, but I hadn't developed a mechanism for using other forms of birth control, like using condoms.

I got pregnant at eighteen. Getting pregnant illuminated a lot about that relationship and, ultimately, ended it. I paid for the abortion myself and I got myself to the clinic and back alone. I was not cold to the emotional impact of the experience. I felt a bit traumatized and a sense of loss. A lot of soul searching went into the decision, even though I knew I didn't want to become a mother at eighteen. It was not the right thing for me; it wasn't what I wanted or was capable of. Still, it would cross my mind: *Oh, it would be three or it would be seven . . .*

I remember wondering, *Should I feel guilty? Should I feel ashamed?* The feelings might have been socially constructed, but emotionally they were real. It took me awhile to really answer those questions, to say to myself, *No, you should not be ashamed. No, you should not allow society to judge your complex responsibilities. Those eggs are yours and what you do with them and which ones you allow to grow is your decision.*

It was a few years before I wrote a song about it, which I think was evidence of my turmoil, because I have never been one to mince words. Writing "Lost Woman Song" was definitely part of a feminist continuum—bringing it out of me in song, speaking out, which was very healing. I don't think I could have written the song without that Lucille Clifton poem called "the lost baby poem."

I had another abortion two years after that first one. I still didn't have my birth control worked out yet without the pill. I was reconfronted with all of those questions: *Now, shouldn't I be ashamed? Wasn't I supposed to have learned that lesson?* To admit to having one is to admit to being young and inexperienced, but to have two, well, you're a bona fide floozy and irresponsible.

It's been fifteen years since I have had an abortion or really written about it, and I'm suddenly realizing that the tools I needed in order to understand having a reproductive system or what it meant to be a horny youth, these tools were not given to me. They were squelched by patriarchal society—women's knowledge and stories were kept from me, even a basic understanding of how common abortion is that could counteract that shaming around it was suppressed. I mean, the idea that you can just "choose" abstinence is false, because our bodies and desires are designed to push us to have sex when we are the most likely to get pregnant—it's all stacked up to get us pregnant.

You know what? I'm thirty-five now and I just found out I'm pregnant a few days ago. I'm having a baby and I'm thrilled. I can't believe I'd ever look on that piss-on-the-stick and feel good about it. I want people to understand that pregnancy is bigger than individual responsibility. I want to tell women and men, "You are an animal and it is a beautiful thing."*

*Ani gave birth to her daughter, Petah Lucia, on January 20, 2007.

SEBASTIANA CORREA, BORN JANUARY 3, 1973

When I read the "I Had an Abortion" piece in the Nation, I felt like a heavy weight just got off of my back. I had an abortion too, and I do not regret I did. Is that selfish?

I came to this country to attend college, and after eighteen months here I went back home to Brazil for summer break and had a wonderful time with my former boyfriend. When I got back I found I was pregnant. I could have left college and gone back home to have this child and maybe never be able to return and finish college—or I could have an abortion. My first reaction was of happiness that I found out I was pregnant in a country where abortion is legal. In my Catholic country, abortion is illegal and immoral. I could never tell my parents about it. My father would have had me killed, literally. My mother was so against abortion, she adopted eight girls from young mothers who wanted to have abortions.

At the time I found out I was pregnant, I was living with a host family, and I was afraid to let them know about it in case they tried to send me home. I tried to tell my closest friend here that I thought I was pregnant, and she called me stupid. So I decided to do it on my own. I called Planned Parenthood, I made an appointment and did it. With no one by my side to hold my hand and with no anesthesia because I had to drive home.

The other day I was in the gym, I heard on TV the president talking about an abortion ban, and I thought this is the biggest step backwards this country can take. I blame a big part of my country's social problems in the lack of a law that supports abortion. All those mothers whose kids are on the streets begging . . . An abortion would not be a sin if abortion were legal. Sin is to bear a child who will become a street beggar, a child who will have to sell his or her body when they are only eight years old in order to have food to eat.

I never spoke of [my abortion] until this letter to you. I felt relief reading about your project because I felt I was not the only one. I feel lucky I was in the U.S. when I was pregnant. I feel really lucky.[*]

---

[*]From the original e-mail that Sebastiana sent me after reading about the abortion project in the *Nation*.

A'YEN TRAN, BORN DECEMBER 10, 1980

When I was nineteen I had an abortion.
My boyfriend and I were living together in Brooklyn, and it
turned out to be a really bad relationship, very isolating . . .

He was an activist and poet like me, and we did everything together. He was wild and fanciful and fun, and we got to be really close, but he was emotionally abusive and he turned sexually abusive. I think the breaking point was . . . well, I would wake up and he was having sex with me, and sometimes choking me. It was horrible.

I was raised by a single mother and we are very close, but I didn't tell my mother until I was having the abortion. I felt reluctant to tell her, not because I was thinking she would say, *Oh, you're doing something wrong,* or, *You should feel guilty for it.* I was afraid she'd be disappointed that I'd gotten myself in trouble—you know, *You screwed up. Be more careful next time.* I went to the doctor's office and I got this shot of methotrexate [a cancer treatment that can be used for inducing abortion] and then went home and inserted some suppositories. That induces—I guess they are contractions—and expels the mass of cells. My boyfriend actually *left* the house and went to a poetry reading while I was going through the abortion. It made it worse to be alone.

As for the actual abortion, I was just lying on my bed, trying to read, when the cramping came on. It was one of the most painful experiences I've ever been through. I just felt like my insides were tearing themselves apart. I felt so alone and I didn't know what to do. At a certain point I even passed out from the pain. When I woke up, I called my mother. She left the dinner she was at to come over and help me. She said, "A'yen, you need to know you can always tell me this as soon as you know and I'm going to be there for you."

It wasn't until the next day that the pain subsided and then the mass itself came out while I was walking down the street. I felt like I had just been through something big, but I didn't question the validity of my actions. In fact, I sort of felt good that I had gone ahead and done what I did. In the subway, right afterwards, there were these ads that said, *Post-abortion trauma? Come see our ministry,* or whatever the hell it was. I was so offended. I wanted to call and say, *I've just had an abortion. I am fine.* I felt like it was so absurd and so offensive that they were trying to coerce people to manufacture feelings of guilt. I didn't feel guilty—I even told my story at an abortion speak-out a few days after the procedure—but I did still feel like there was a wall of silence around it, in a way.

For instance, I'm one of the leaders of this big Students for Choice club at Columbia University. It's this huge club, there are tons of us in it, yet you don't really hear people coming out and talking about having an abortion. People are willing to put up flyers and go to marches and come clinic escort-ing with us, but . . . the air of openness that I sort of expect isn't really there. I didn't feel like I could just tell people, and it seemed really inappropriate to be open about it even in that obviously welcoming circumstance.

I had a second abortion in 2003. I was dating this wonderful, wonderful person. We had an incredibly supportive relationship and I had women in my life who were supportive. At Barnard, the health services policy is really sen-sitive to abortion, and to all needs of women. You go to a very welcoming and soft private practice with a very nice doctor. The first abortion experience had been sort of negative, but this experience—the doctor and her assistant, I didn't feel like I was just being operated on. I felt like they were looking at me and I was connecting. This was a suction "surgical" abortion. It took five minutes. It was intense but not incredibly painful. It was a pinprick kind of feeling, and then a kind of intense sucking feeling, but then it was over. As soon as it was over, they brought my boyfriend in and he held my hand. I recovered for a few minutes and then we went home.

I really think it works the same for both sexual assault and abortion. The silence is the worst part. Now that I've had an abortion, I feel like it's incred-ibly important for me to be able to speak about it and for me to encourage people around me to feel comfortable speaking about it.[*]

[*]From an interview conducted by Gillian Aldrich in 2004.

ROBIN RINGLEKA, BORN JUNE 10, 1974

*When I was eighteen, my Catholic high school organized
a trip with the diocese in Memphis to go to the annual
Roe v. Wade protest in D.C. . . .*

My friend's mother had exposed me to peaceful pro-life marches in Memphis and I thought this national one would be even better.

My mother is pro-choice. In fact, I was very hesitant to ask her if I could go because she's an ardent feminist who has always been very open and vocal about her pro-choice stance. At that age I really railed against my mother and her alternative ideas. She had lesbian relationships for ten years but wasn't entirely comfortable with her sexuality. I picked up on this anxiety and internalized it to a large extent myself. We had moved from Michigan to Tennessee when I was twelve (two years after she came out), and it proved to be a major culture shock for our whole family. My mother would bring pseudo-dates to my school functions because she wasn't really out to the rest of the world. I always felt like a freak because everybody at my school had this grand normalcy—or at least I imagined that they did. When I was exposed to Catholicism, I welcomed and latched on pretty tightly. As odd as it may sound, I think it's fair to say that I "rebelled" with religion. I was certain my mom didn't want me to go to the protest, but she surprised me when she said, "If you feel strongly enough about something that you need to march on Washington, I'll fund the trip."

The night before the march, they had a special mass in honor of the annual pro-life pilgrimage to D.C. The basilica in D.C. is just breathtaking and it was teeming with people who had traveled from across the United States to attend the march. I remember being surprised at the number of men there, it seemed like most of the participants were male. The chaperones on the trip really emphasized what a privilege this was for us—there were going to be bishops and cardinals from all over the world here. At one point early in the mass I heard this blood-curdling scream from the back of the church that resounded throughout the basilica. A woman was screaming about these men and their attempts to control women and end legalized abortion. I instinctively turned to acknowledge the source of the screams, but the priest next to me grabbed ahold of me so that I couldn't physically turn around. Perhaps they are used to this kind of thing happening at such gatherings, but I was so affected that I began to cry. I noticed another young woman close by who seemed equally as freaked out, and she was crying too.

At the march the next day, I was lost in a sea of really graphic images. We had talked about abortion in religion class at length—and especially about all of the Christian families with good homes waiting for children while selfish women aborted their babies—but I had never seen anything like this. Amid pictures of dismembered fetuses, there was a woman with a happy, chubby little white baby. My friends and I posed for pictures with the infant because we thought it seemed so appropriate. I felt like the trip was important and invigorating. My pro-life stance was a significant part of my identity, as was my commitment to save sex until marriage.

Dennis didn't go to my school. I knew who he was because my sister had gone to his school and he was really beautiful and popular. We both worked at the mall—I worked at Lerner and he worked at Gadzooks. We talked here and there when we would see each other on our lunch breaks, and soon we were dating. Every time we slept together I would promise myself that it wasn't going to happen again, because my shame was so great. I believed that pregnancy only happened to a certain type of girl, and we would protect ourselves only some of the time. But of course I wouldn't plan ahead, because to do so would mean that I had intentions, and I didn't want to be that kind of girl either.

In July of 1992 I suspected I was pregnant. I was sick almost right away. I told Dennis that I didn't believe in abortion and if I were pregnant we'd have to put the child up for adoption. We bought two pregnancy tests and they were both positive. I was very ashamed, first and foremost, and scared of what people would think. I felt like a jerk and a fraud, especially because I had been so vocal (and self-righteous) about waiting until marriage. You could say that I had a lot riding on the identity I'd created, and there was no way to hide a pregnancy. One of my primary concerns, if not the biggest, was keeping this whole business under wraps, and going far away to have a baby really appealed to me.

We had learned in religion class about a baby shortage and I sincerely believed that there were all of these families waiting with open arms. I found an agency out east that placed babies with affluent families. The woman with whom I spoke was really great, and she commended me for my bravery. We talked at length, and she told me about the wonderful opportunities babies placed through their program would have. The agency had these portfolios with glossy photos from which I could choose adoptive parents to interview. She said that I could even start taking college classes and that I wouldn't have to worry about expenses while I lived in Boston. She asked about my background and my plans for college in the fall. I had a cheerleading scholarship to the University of Tennessee. She said there was no reason that I couldn't go back the following year after I gave birth and just "pick up where I left off," cheerleading and all. It didn't even occur to me that going through pregnancy and giving up a child for adoption might be hard on me.

Then she asked about Dennis. I told her about his athletic scholarship to Brigham Young and the good family from which he came. I remember feeling sort of nervous talking about him but pushed these feelings down. I must have indicated he wasn't white because she stopped me and said, "Oh, so Dennis is black?" I could tell right away something horrible was happening. When I said yes, she said, "Oh, well . . . I'm very sorry but our program can't help you. There just isn't demand for biracial children."

I hung up and thought, *Oh my God. I'm going to have to stay in this community. I'm going to have a child at eighteen. Not only am I going to have a child, but a biracial child.* I can't even tell you the hostility with which Dennis and I were met in Memphis and we didn't even hold hands in public. I couldn't imagine how this child would be treated, how I'd be treated.

Dennis and I started looking for other options. We first went to a place that was advertising "all options" counseling. Before we walked in, I recognized the sticker on their door from my days of protesting and recognized it as a pro-life crisis pregnancy center. I didn't go in. I must have known that I was seriously considering terminating the pregnancy and if I went in there, I was just going to be traumatized. I remember thinking that I could now understand how tempted women were to end their pregnancies, and realized it was time to talk to my mom.

My mother was initially calm, but told me it was outrageous to think that I could go to school and be pregnant at the same time, and that she would not support me and this child. An abortion was the only answer. She told me that she, too, had terminated a pregnancy, but would not discuss the details (and to this day never has). At the time I was really angry at her for saying she wouldn't support me, or at least I pretended to be. But honestly, I think I was immensely relieved. I had zero interest in being a mother, but I was not ready to admit to myself that I really wanted to terminate this pregnancy. I allowed her response to "let me off the hook" and blamed it on her, asserting that I had no other choice. And so I "agreed" to have an abortion.

The day of the abortion, I remember my sister driving into the clinic entrance and saying, "Oh my God, don't look!" Of course I looked and there were protesters everywhere. There was this really crazed-looking older man storming back and forth in front of the entrance, pushing a baby carriage and hollering. The protesters didn't block our way, but were close enough to really upset me by the time I could be whisked in through the back entrance.

The doctor was very rushed and didn't have much of a bedside manner. I was pretty terrified and I began to cry when he entered the room. This seemed to piss him off and he demanded to know why I was crying. I started thinking really fast. I knew that this needed to happen and I had to pull myself together and get it over with. I said, "Oh, I'm fine. I'm just a little scared." There was a doctor's assistant present who must have been through this with many, many women—or perhaps through it herself—because nobody at the clinic had seemed especially nice until her. She was very reassuring and calm, and held my hand while I cried and drifted into sleep. I woke up in another room with a pad in my underpants. I checked the pad and saw blood. I remember thinking that this may result in eternal damnation—but more than anything else, I felt immense relief and offered up a prayer of thanks.

The first person I told (other than my dad) was a guy I was dating at college freshman year. He really couldn't have been a worse candidate to date or tell, but I think by that point I was into punishing myself. The one-year anniversary of my abortion was approaching and I was having bad dreams. One of these nights I awoke and told him everything. He screamed and threw things but, honestly, he was more offended that I had slept with a black guy than that I had an abortion. He proceeded to tell his friends what had happened. They would say things like, "Man, we can't believe that you even touch her," and then he would bring that up in fights. I didn't stay with him much longer after that.

I didn't talk about it again until I had transferred from University of Tennessee to Michigan State University. My best friend, Shannon, had taken a Women's Studies class and encouraged me to enroll. I did, and then another, and I was hooked. Around the same time I found a therapist that I really liked named Terri.

I had reached a point in therapy where I knew I couldn't progress any further until I told Terri about my abortion. But I was terrified of her reaction nonetheless and didn't know where to begin. I began to cry and told her that there was something so horrible that I had done and couldn't figure out how to tell her. I knew that she had lost a baby hours after he was born; I think that was why I was so afraid to tell her. I told her, "Maybe I'd feel better if you could tell me how Nicholas died."

Then *she* started to cry and she said, "Oh, honey. You've had an abortion, haven't you?"—I was so relieved that she said it for me. Then she said, "Robin, I've had one too." I was floored.

"You don't understand," I said, "it's not just the abortion but the circumstances surrounding it." At this point I was really crying hard. "I don't know if I'm as dedicated to antiracism as I'd like myself, and others, to believe."

And so I told her the story about how I had an abortion after I was told it couldn't be adopted and how I had been scared to be eighteen and have a biracial kid in Memphis (or any kid, anywhere!) and I didn't want to be a mother then anyway.

Terri was so angry on my behalf. She said, "You had no idea how complex this issue was. You were told your baby wasn't wanted. You weren't supported, Robin." She encouraged me to tell Shannon.

We had lived together for a couple of years and I had never been that close to anyone. I poured the whole story out while she held my hand. I was so scared of what her reaction might be, that she might go so far as to kick me out of the house.

When I stopped talking long enough to take a breath, Shannon said, "I would never judge you and I love you and this explains all of the shame that you carry around with you—because it never made sense to me before."

After Shannon, I began telling my close friends one by one. With every person I told I became more confident, angry, and unapologetic. I wasn't looking for forgiveness anymore. I was looking to debunk the dangerous myths that surround abortion and the women who seek them. I am an advocate for keeping abortion safe and legal, and also for women having good information about our bodies and our options so that we can make informed decisions.

One of my biggest issues with the pro-life movement is the racism implicit in their arguments against abortion. Unlike what I learned in religion class, worldwide there isn't a "baby shortage." In our own country there isn't either. To say there is a baby shortage is to suggest that nonwhite babies aren't babies. According to the Guttmacher Institute, there are over 586,000 children in the U.S. alone without homes, 100,000 of whom are available right now for adoption. *Right now.* And many of these are children of color. And then add to that all of the children born into abusive families and environments that don't want or honor or nurture them.

I have come to believe that having an abortion can be a very motherly decision. I am not sorry that I had an abortion. I am only sorry that I was duped by antichoice rhetoric, about my brief role in perpetuating it, and that so much of my time and energy was spent feeling shameful and fearful of my story and sexuality. I am profoundly grateful for my experience with an unintended pregnancy. It has been a gift that has transformed my worldview and made me a more compassionate and dedicated advocate for women, children, and choice.

JENNY EGAN, BORN SEPTEMBER 5, 1980

I'm one of five children in a Mormon family. My father is a marine, Republican, Mormon lawyer. I was raised in a church where abortion was a horror and something that was not acceptable . . .

It's not okay for me and it's not okay for people that I know. I was sixteen when I got pregnant. It was with my boyfriend. The first time we had sex it wasn't completely consensual. He would sort of accuse me of being a lesbian and—though it turned out he was on to something—in my high school world at that time, it was easier to have sex I didn't want than to be called a lesbian. I had this detachment for the next couple of weeks where we had sex a couple more times and I was very passive—and traumatized and upset—so I had unprotected sex probably four times that month. I thought after the second time that I might be pregnant, but then I had some spotting and I thought that I had my period and that I was fine. Later that month, though, my breasts swelled up and I just knew, I knew immediately.

God, the panic of picturing my life! I was surrounded by teenage pregnancy and by poverty in Tangent, the small town in Oregon where I was raised. I am the daughter of a teenage mother, who's the daughter of a teenage mother. I went to my boyfriend's house. At that point, he had already become very detached from the situation and from me as a person—he was intently watching wrestling and playing video games.

I did not tell my parents. I kept imagining scenarios where I would tell them and they were all very horrifying. I went with my boyfriend and friend to Planned Parenthood. I think I was headed into my eighth week at that point. I went to a room for pre-abortion counseling—five quick, terse questions. I had assumed that I was going to get a half-hour and I would finally be able to tell someone or talk to someone about how freaked out I was, but I didn't get to. And I remember being upset about that. And then I went in for the procedure and the doctor was actually the most comforting presence of all. She looked me in the eye and allowed me to talk more than anyone had up until that point. And I felt immediately better. The procedure was so short! I was amazed at how short it was. It was slightly painful—probably like the worst cramps that I ever had.

My boyfriend started the breaking-up process the day after the abortion. He said he wanted to date other people. I was traumatized because I thought he was the only person I could talk to in the world about this pregnancy and abortion because he had experienced it with me.

Two weeks after I had my procedure, I came home from school and my mother was holding a letter. She was shaking and had this very blank expression on her face. My first instinct was to turn around and run, but before I could, she said: "Sit the fuck down, your dad's on his way."

I thought, *If my dad's coming home from work, that's a problem.* I sat down, I was already crying, and she threw this letter in my lap. It was an eight-by-eleven piece of paper and there was this silhouette of three men in the corner, and it said, *The Brotherhood*—that was the stationery. It addressed both my parents by their full names and then it said: *Your daughter Jennifer had an abortion on April 9, 1997. Please let God guide your actions from this point forward.* Signed, *The Brotherhood.*

My mother yelled: "Did you do this!?"

I said, "Yes."

My dad came home about that time. He's sort of the stern person in the family. I was too big but he wrapped me up into a little ball, and I was sobbing uncontrollably, and he just held me and said, "It's okay, Jenny, it's okay, it's okay."

My mom at that point was screaming and yelling: "I can't believe you would do this! You killed your baby . . ."

My dad told me he thought I should just leave. I had never been able to leave my house without saying where I was going. And it was just all of a sudden they're not caring enough to know where I was going . . . *asking* me to leave the house in that condition. I took painkillers and sleeping pills that day. I couldn't imagine going back to my house, and I couldn't imagine having my mother call me a murderer again. But I did return home after a few hours, and we never really talked about it again.

Everything about my home was now marked and tainted by the abortion and I was very determined to get away. So I sort of pulled my life together and applied to college very far away. I went to an all-women's college, Smith, where the rhetoric about abortion and the talk of pregnancy was so different. I had never heard of anyone talking about abortion. I had never heard anyone say that they had an abortion. I assumed, telling someone, that they would be as judgmental or as disappointed in me as I was in myself for getting pregnant. And it was just this amazing thing to have someone hug me and say, "I'm so sorry you went through that." That was it, and to have them completely unfazed by me telling them was so heartening.

I do feel a lot more open about it in the last couple of years, and I think that's mostly related to me losing my guilt. And losing some of my surety that I had done some harm or that I had done something bad. And as that started to fall away, talking about it became increasingly important.

I know now that there are adult women in my life who have had abortions. But if any of them had been open about it, if I could have gone to talk to one person who would have experienced it, I think it would have changed those years of guilt and shame for me.

CHAPTER 6

LET'S TALK

My friend Marion Banzhaf is not only the kind of gutsy broad who wears an *I had an abortion* T-shirt, she also has *LET'S TALK* scrawled by hand beneath the message. To Marion, reproductive health and freedom come through directness and inviting open conversation. Working at feminist health centers throughout the 1970s, she demonstrated vaginal self-exams and performed menstrual extractions. She was a pioneering member of the AIDS activist group ACT UP, and she recounts the story of her abortion both in this book and in the film *I Had an Abortion*. To recap: The year of her unintended pregnancy was 1971, and there were only a couple of states where abortion was legal. She raised the money for her procedure in one afternoon by standing on her college campus's quad, asking for donations. She then flew from Gainesville, Florida to New York City, had her procedure, and, after she left the clinic, ran skipping down the street. "I was so happy to see that blood," she says about the abortion, in a trademark Marion Banzhaf way (somewhat shocking, totally confident). "I felt like my life was beginning over again."

Dauntless radical though she is, there is a part of her abortion story she rarely tells. A year after her 1971 procedure, Marion got pregnant again. This time she didn't have to worry about the money. Her new boyfriend pulled out his checkbook and put her on the next flight to New York—and she knew it was the right decision. "But it was a much harder [abortion] for me personally. I felt I shouldn't [have] let myself get pregnant [again]. Even to this day, I have shame about it. An accomplished, consciousness-raised feminist like me!"

One abortion, that happens. Two? Well, to paraphrase Oscar Wilde's Lady Bracknell, two sounds like carelessness. Abortion itself (whether your first or fourth) is so shrouded in secrecy, it's easy to imagine that only certain kinds of women would ever make a mistake like that *twice*. If she does, this almost unconscious thinking goes, it's clear she doesn't care enough to have learned from the first one. Fears about these repeat cases contribute to the idea that since terminating a pregnancy is legal, women may use abortion as birth control. (As in the oft-heard remark, "I'm pro-choice, but I don't think women should use it for birth control.")

The Guttmacher Institute estimates that "if a sexually active woman were to use abortion as her means of birth control and wanted two children, she would have about thirty abortions by the time she reached age forty-five." By contrast, the more typical number of repeats is two or three—hardly constituting a disavowal of responsible contraception. (Two out of every one hundred women aged fifteen to forty-four will have an abortion this year, and half of them have had at least one abortion previously, according to the Guttmacher Institute.) "You have 300 possibilities to get pregnant in your life," says Peg Johnston, the aforementioned director of Southern Tier Women's Services, an abortion clinic just outside Binghamton, New York. "A one-percent failure rate—assuming the best possible use of contraception—is still *three* abortions," she says. "In what endeavor is a one-percent failure rate not acceptable?" Sensible, it's true—and yet virtually every woman I have talked to about multiple abortions felt she shouldn't have let it happen again, implying it was her fault.

Why is that? Well, some of it surely reflects a robust pro-life movement that, when abortion became legal, mobilized to scream at women opting for the procedure. But it's not *just* a vast right-wing conspiracy. Many pro-choice women believe that abortion is taking a life (if not a truly independent life). What justifies that loss of life is the woman's *own* life. It's almost as if she is saying, "I recognize that this is serious, but my own life is too important to sacrifice for an unplanned pregnancy." Each additional abortion makes it harder to believe she is making an honorable decision.

Or that *he* is. My friend Matt, like many men in my life, has been part of more than one abortion. When he was younger, he was "knee-jerk pro-choice." If an unplanned pregnancy occurs in high school or college, he figured, of course you have an abortion. That's just common sense. He didn't revisit that line of thinking with any sort of introspection until the first abortion. "I wasn't in love, we had no future together, I was comfortable saying we need to abort," Matt concludes. "I gave her money. She didn't express any need for me to be there with her."

He describes, bluntly, how a recent abortion felt "more like murder," and how he was disgusted at himself for putting his partner in the position of being confronted by scary protesters and having to endure such an awful day. The circumstances were different—Matt's future with this woman appeared promising—yet having a baby just then, a few months into their relationship, still didn't seem like a good idea. "I sat at the clinic with all of these younger guys and I thought, *I am too old to be here,*" says Matt, thirty-seven at the time of that second abortion. "*When do I stop giving myself the out?* That is what abortion feels like—a free pass. But it's not totally free, there are emotional consequences, and as you get older the sense of taking responsibility for your actions grows." Like with Marion, the shame for Matt was not the abortion itself, it was the shame of the pregnancy. As one interviewee put it, "Getting accidentally pregnant means that you don't have enough control and power to take care of yourself"—or the person you love.

Which brings us to a paradox of feminism. The success of the women's movement is not just in its overhaul of the institutions that have traditionally kept women subjugated. The more profound revolution is the raised expectations this once-utopian movement suggests to its daughters. The mantra of empowerment means that women feel like responsible actors in sex, and that knowledge makes it harder, in a way, to justify the "mistake" of unplanned pregnancy, even if they know that all birth control has a fail-ure rate and that intercourse with a man always caries a risk of pregnancy.

The *I Had an Abortion* film ends with dozens of women saying, "My name is ____ and I had an abortion." A few say, "I had two abortions." One woman says, "I had three abortions," and at an early screening her presence pro-voked one young female audience member to wonder aloud why the woman didn't use birth control and should we, the filmmakers, be promoting the idea that multiple abortions were as justified as a single one? A well-known second-wave feminist who was also at the screening, writer Alix Kates Shul-man, replied that she'd had *four* abortions—"and not one was the result of carelessness." A few audience members vigorously nodded their heads in support, but it looked as if most people were undecided on this question.

At another screening, Pauline Bart, a second-wave feminist, suggested that younger women learn to perform abortions themselves just as the Jane Collective had done pre–*Roe v. Wade*. "It's just like taking a melon-baller and scooping out a melon," she said. I nodded earnestly but thought, *No, it isn't*. Or, at least, it isn't to me. I don't doubt that some women experience abortion as devoid of angst as Pauline Bart depicts, and for them each abor-tion is created equal. For many women, however, an unintended pregnancy is a painful mistake. The mistake is often not solely or even primarily your own fault—Alix Kates Shulman was not told by her doctor that diaphragms could slip out of place; Marion Banzhaf got depressed on the high-dose pill and found it almost impossible to take. Fertility and sexuality are very com-plex and, let's be real, some people are better at birth control than others. I've had unprotected sex more often than protected sex myself, so I'm hardly one to *tsk-tsk*. Many women in this book feel like we don't ever have real control over getting pregnant—as Ani DiFranco says, "You are an animal, and that is a beautiful thing."

On the other hand, virtually everyone I have spoken to who has worked in a clinic has a story of a patient who had more than a dozen abortions, despite contraceptive counseling with each clinic visit. Peg Johnston, a clinician with thirty years experience, thinks multiple abortions on that scale usually happen in the context of a life out of control in other ways. Often it's a woman who has several children already and a chaotic, stressful life. A history of sexual abuse can also play out in the life of a woman not taking care of herself in matters of birth control. Sadly, though, the most common factor here is that at around thirty to fifty dollars a month for the pill, many women can't afford their birth control. A majority of the forty-five million uninsured in this country are women. Another longtime clinic director, Claire Keyes of Allegheny Reproductive Health Center in Pittsburgh, told me that for many women with insurance covering birth control, their policies mandate generic pills, which only have to contain eighty percent of the ingredients in brand-name birth control. This weaker dose is diluted even more when you consider the escalating average weights of women today—and both are largely unanalyzed contributions to birth control failures. Meanwhile, Johnston continues, "Some people are really fertile and others simply have lots and lots of sex. Frankly, if you have a lot of sex, you'll get pregnant more often."

Marion Banzhaf with her *Talk to Me* philosophy definitely cops to having had lots of sex, but for the last thirty years this has been primarily with women. When Banzhaf was becoming a conscious adult in the late 1960s, she didn't yet know what a lesbian was. Feminists protesting the Miss America Pageant in 1968 made the TV news in her hometown of Sarasota, Florida, but the Stonewall Rebellion—where drag queens fought back against bigoted raids of a gay bar—most definitely did not. "I had never heard the word lesbian, never met someone who said they were a lesbian," recalls Banzhaf. "What I knew was that I liked to hang out with my girlfriends more than with guys, but I also knew that my preference wasn't normal—I knew I should like boys." Determined to normalize herself, Banzhaf found a boy to "devirginate" her the summer before she went to college. "I was working at a summer camp and had a relationship with another counselor." Amid all of the normalizing she was trying to do, it didn't even occur to her to ask about birth control, but fortunately, her chosen partner used a condom.

According to a 1999 report by the Guttmacher Institute, "Bisexual and lesbian respondents were almost as likely as heterosexual women to at some point have had male-female intercourse (thirty-three percent and twenty-nine percent, respectively), but they had a significantly higher prevalence of pregnancy (twelve percent) and physical or sexual abuse (nineteen to twenty-two percent) than heterosexual or unsure adolescents." Jenny Egan, born in 1980, describes her early sexual experiences as coercive:

I had various inklings as a teenager, but I definitely identified as straight. At the same time, from a sort of young age, I had various people in my life ask me if I was gay. I was this wannabe punk rock kid—I wore suit jackets, for crying out loud. My boyfriend at that time would always say, "Are you sure you're not gay?" Because of those questions, I often put myself in dangerous situations. I would certainly characterize myself as sexually promiscuous. I would get into situations with over-masculine dangerous characters and think, This will prove what a normal, straight woman I am. I couldn't always choose whether to have sex. There were times that I recall when I would resist my boyfriend's sexual attention and he would accuse me of being a dyke, so suddenly I was in this position where either I was going to have sex that I didn't want to have or I was a dyke. For sixteen-year-old me, it was better to have the unwanted sex.

Jenny got pregnant in one of those not-quite-consensual situations and, for her, it's clear that queer identity (or fear of it) at a young age can lead to the kind of sexual coercion from which feminists have long fought to protect women. Egan argues that homophobia thereby creates sexual abuse, rather than sexual abuse creating a gay person. High-risk behavior can be the result of feeling the need to prove a femininity associated with heterosexuality—and is one of the many links between queer women and abortion rights. In essence, reproductive freedom and sexual liberation are inextricable from one another; autonomy and equality for women presumes both.

In September 1989, during the height of the AIDS crisis, Banzhaf wrote an article for *OutWeek* about the importance of reproductive rights for queer people. Around the same time, an influential pamphlet began circulating in her activist crowd entitled, "In Our Own Hands: Sisters Doing It for Themselves—Safe Self Abortion." "We circulated it within the queer community," explains Banzhaf, to make the statement that "lesbians need to know this just as much as straight woman." She also pioneered the promotion of contraceptive use among queer women.

The woman who became "Jane Roe" perhaps most embodies the thicket of complex issues that have always surrounded reproductive rights. In addition to never having had an abortion, another counterintuitive detail of Norma McCorvey's life is that she spent most of it as a woman "who loves women," as she put it in her 1994 autobiography, *I Am Roe* (written with Andy Meisler). As a wild preteen in Dallas, she robbed a Texaco station and used the money to run away with her best friend, holing up in a Oklahoma City motel and making love with her. A few years later, Norma was sent to reform school in Gainesville, Texas, where "a pack of cigarettes would get you an empty room for an hour"; she had girlfriends galore. Finally, around 1970, she met Connie Gonzales, the woman with whom she would spend most of her life. Despite the fact that Norma "openly lived a lesbian lifestyle," she did have at least a few male lovers, resulting in her three children. The person upon whom legalized abortion is built was a queer woman seeking to terminate an unwanted, unplanned pregnancy.

Norma "was her own kind of feminist," according to Meisler. She was not only queer, but a carnie, poor, undereducated, and had substance abuse problems. "At the time that [attorney] Sarah Weddington was looking for a plaintiff," says Meisler, "anyone without Norma's problems, any middle-class woman who was educated," would have known where to go to get an abortion. "Norma was bitter about that," he says. "She used to call them the Vassar girls."

Norma was fifteen years old, a rough-around-the-edges former reform school student with a string of girlfriends in her past, when she met, and in short order married, Woody McCorvey, and then moved with him to Los Angeles. They didn't use birth control, and when Norma soon became pregnant, Woody beat the living daylights out of her. It wasn't the first time, and feeling the swell of another life in her body, Norma decided to escape her feckless husband and head back to Texas to live with her mother. It wasn't the easiest choice. Her mother had always put men before Norma, and in fact it was her mother who had sent Norma off to reform school. Nonetheless, Norma went home, had her baby—a girl she named Melissa—and began trying to care for her.

Within a few months of her daughter's birth, Norma sought a bit of a social life. Her time with Woody hadn't been so great, and she headed to the one lesbian bar she knew of in Dallas. When her mother realized that Norma was fooling around with women, she kicked her out of the house and, in a tricky maneuver, coerced her into signing over the rights to her daughter. In *I Am Roe*, Norma expresses devastation about losing rights to her daughter:

> *The world is often very confusing to me, and the rules seem to shift with whoever is following them, but of one thing I am absolutely certain: leaving Melissa with my mother was the worst thing I have ever done . . . To some people, an eighteen-year-old lesbian waitress might not have seemed like a good mother for a baby. But these people never knew the love I had, and still have, for Melissa . . . I will take that sorrow to my grave.*

A couple of years later, while working as an orderly at a hospital, Norma had an affair with a coworker and got pregnant again. This time she never even saw the baby after giving birth, just signed the papers so that the girl could be adopted. At twenty-two, Norma had another brief heterosexual affair—this time with a hustler with whom she played pool—and found she was pregnant yet again. Distraught and depressed, Norma was sure that she didn't want to bring another baby into the world, just to have to give it

up once more. Desperate, she sought an abortion, making a visit to an illegal clinic that had been busted just days before, begging the doctor who
had delivered her babies to help her. Finally, someone referred her to two
young lawyers aiming to challenge the Texas law banning abortions. She met
with them in a Dallas pizza parlor and agreed to become the plaintiff in *Roe
v. Wade*, not understanding (or perhaps not being informed) that the legal
battle would not be decided in time for her to get an abortion.

The *Roe* baby was born in 1970. The nurses treated Norma like a baby
machine, not a mother, injecting her with a shot to dry up her milk. Meanwhile, hospital administrators threatened her with an astronomical bill that
she would have to pay if she didn't go through with the adoption. Another
nurse then brought Norma's daughter to her, plopped her on Norma's chest,
and said, "Feeding time!" with a smile. "It was like getting a glimpse of hell—
all of my shame and fear and guilt and love and sadness all rolled up into a
ball and placed in front of me," wrote Norma. "There was a flap of cloth over
[her daughter's] face. My entire body, my entire soul cried out to me to turn
the flap down, to look at my baby's face. But my mind told me that it would
be [the] worst thing that I could ever do." Soon after leaving the hospital
and surrendering this third daughter, Norma tried to commit suicide. Two
years later, she learned about the *Roe* victory.

Norma McCorvey's conversion to pro-life politics was a complex process.
She was the kind of woman for whom unplanned pregnancy came with few
options. Her role in the *Roe* victory was passive. Her inclusion in the pro-
choice community of the '70s and '80s was awkward, as she'd had no experience of abortion. Plus, with her drug addiction and lesbian life, she wasn't
the ideal good girl to represent the cause. There was little McCorvey had to
show for her vaunted contribution to choice, and having given birth to three
children, it no doubt stung to never be acknowledged as a mother. She gave
those daughters life, and yet since she didn't raise them, that role of gestation
and birth is perhaps all she has to hold on to.

"Abortion is often portrayed as the cause of social ills," Merle Hoffman, a longtime abortion advocate, told me. "But abortion is the *effect* of social inequalities"—like hopelessness, poverty, and rape—"not the cause." If we care about reducing the need for abortion, we have to commit ourselves to the broadest, most inclusive social justice agenda. We have to care about poor people, gay people, people of color, and we have to be willing to build the support networks, education, and respect that can truly have an impact on "dangerous sexual situations." We have to value the experiences of the birth mothers like Norma McCorvey.

On the surface, Marion and Norma are similar. Both came of age in the '60s in Southern conservative environments. They both faced unplanned pregnancies and discovered they loved women, yet they had such different paths—Marion found the information and resources and support she needed to have a semblance of control over her life, and Norma did not.

At the end of the day, feminism is not about what choice you make, it's about having the *ability* to make a choice. Norma McCorvey and so many other women have been and continue to be deprived of this right. That is why Norma's story, including her pro-life conversion, is not a threat to the cause of abortion rights; her story *is* our cause.

TRUTH TO POWER

At the very beginning of the "I Had an Abortion" project, Gloria Steinem told me about sitting with a fifty-something friend who was a staunch supporter of abortion rights. This friend was extremely frustrated and worried about her daughter, whom she thought wasn't sufficiently anxious about the fragility of reproductive rights. "She doesn't know what it would be like to not have access to a legal abortion," fumed the friend. "I *know*. I went through the humiliation and terror of finding an illegal abortion in the '60s."

"So you talk to your daughter about your experiences," said Gloria, "and she just doesn't get it?"

"Oh no," countered the friend, "I've never told her my story. I talk to her about the *issue!*"

Another day months later, while working on this book, my assistant Constance revealed to me that while she worked tirelessly on abortion rights, she wasn't aware of anyone closer to her having had a procedure. We agreed it was odd, but left it there. After hearing the above story, Constance decided to ask her mother if anyone in her family had ever had an abortion. "Actually, *I* had an abortion," replied her mother. "Five years ago. You were in high school. I didn't want to tell you." Constance was flabbergasted. She had talked with her mother about lawmakers' views, Supreme Court cases, and

RU-486 countless times. But her mother had never placed herself inside the issue until Constance asked her directly.

More than three decades after women secured abortion rights, we still build walls too frequently between our politics and our lives. We can shout our politics from the treetops, but we have a hard time believing that our own lives might provide the best road map to strengthening women's reproductive freedoms.

Inga Muscio, the author of the contemporary feminist classic *Cunt: A Declaration of Independence* (1998), was the first person I ever met who a) admitted to multiple abortions, and b) said the surgical solution, in her words, "sucked." In her writings, she recounts two clinic-based vacuum aspiration abortions that she found unpleasant both emotionally and physically. After Muscio discovered herself pregnant a third time, she vowed not to go back to the clinic and "waltz with the abhorrent machine." Instead, she began talking to her friends, asking around about alternatives, and she learned about the various herbs that have been known to induce abortion (though are not guaranteed), such as pennyroyal, blue cohosh, and wild carrot. She also turned to a friend who was a masseuse, who came to her house each night and massaged her uterus and did reflexology on her feet. She continuously imagined the lining of her uterus shedding, and eight days after she began trying to organically induce a miscarriage, her "embryo plopped on the bathroom floor." Muscio's detailed descriptions of her experiences aren't riddled with shame, but certainly indicate room for improvement when it comes to the clinical abortion experience.

Visiting many clinics in recent years, I've become concerned with how stark and unwelcoming some of them are. While trivial, I believe this reinforces the subconscious message that one's abortion experience *should* be punitive. Certainly the cold procedure rooms, blank waiting room walls (or worse, cheesy posters), and worn furnishings probably don't make patients feel nurtured. (Of course, "if we're worrying about what color the walls are," says Merle Hoffman, "we've come a long way." Touché.)

Further, some of the protocol at clinics has no root in medical care and undermines the comfort of the patient—none perhaps more than the rule many clinics follow that men (or partners, since it could be a female friend or relative or lover) can go no further than the waiting room. Nearly 1.3 million women have abortion procedures each year in the United States, with an estimated 600,000 men standing by their sides. Men are often overlooked when it comes to discussing abortion. This is wrongheaded on several fronts, but mostly because it fails to acknowledge that men are a key part of almost every abortion experience.

Several organizations, spearheaded by forward-thinking clinics, are providing information and support to both women *and* men, and inviting men into the procedure room. Claire Keyes, director of Allegheny Reproductive Health Center in East Liberty, Pennsylvania, is collaborating with Arthur Shostak (a professor at Drexel University and the creator of menandabortion.com) to try and make the clinic experience more inclusive of male partners. At this writing, seven clinics are participating in the initiative—all of them independent.

Historically, there have been many reasons to keep the clinic experience woman-focused. The first clinics grew out of a radical feminist community that was correcting the dominant medical mode that made women largely invisible. Even today, it is sometimes important to talk to a woman separate from her partner or parent to make sure that she is seeking this abortion primarily of her own volition.

I believe in understanding our past—our family history and our movement history—but we can't stay stuck there. One dynamic that remains true regardless of era is that abortions always happen within a deeply personal context. As quoted in a January 2007 speech by Backline's Grayson Dempsey, Dr. George Tiller of Wichita, Kansas (perhaps the most famous provider of later-term abortions) says: "Abortion is not a cerebral or a reproductive issue. Abortion is a matter of the heart . . . [U]ntil one understands the heart of a woman, nothing else about abortion makes any sense at all."

So, how do we engage on a deeper level with such a complex, evolving set of circumstances?

We move forward, as Gloria Steinem says, by telling the truth about what has happened to us, something this books aims to do in a small way. Women coming out of their homes and leaving behind their isolation—speaking up—have motivated almost all the big leaps in reproductive rights.

"What would happen if one woman told the truth about her life?" asked the late poet Muriel Rukeyser. Her answer? "The world would split open."

Similarly, popular musician and activist Ani DiFranco, who has a strong appreciation of the taboos surrounding abortion, wrote a song lyric that refers to the single cell that is an egg: "To split yourself in two is just the most radical thing you can do." Life begins in that split—transformative energy is released into the aperture. Then Ani adds: "So girl if that shit ain't up to you, then you simply are not free."

RESOURCE GUIDE

KEY MOMENTS IN THE HISTORY OF ABORTION RIGHTS

1776 The United States of America is founded. Based on English common law, abortion is legal until quickening—the point when a pregnant woman is able to perceive movement of the fetus.

1821 Connecticut becomes the first state to impose restrictions on abortion. By the turn of the nineteenth century, there is not a single state without an antiabortion statute.

1916 Margaret Sanger opens her first clinic in the Brownsville section of Brooklyn, New York, helping to launch the birth control movement.

1962 Sherri Finkbine, the popular host of children's TV show *Romper Room*, is refused a medically therapeutic abortion in her Arizona hometown. She travels to Sweden and obtains a procedure, raising consciousness about the dire need to liberalize abortion laws in the U.S.

1965 *Griswold v. Connecticut* makes it legal for married couples to obtain birth control, based on the constitutional right to marital privacy.

1970 Hawaii becomes the first state to repeal abortion laws, followed by New York, Alaska, and Washington that same year.

1972 *Eisenstadt v. Baird* makes it legal for unmarried women to obtain birth control.

1973 *Roe v. Wade* makes abortion legal in all fifty states (subject to state restrictions in the last two trimesters of pregnancy), finding that the right to privacy is protected by the due process clause of the Fourteenth Amendment to the Constitution. *Doe v. Bolton* strikes down a Georgia law that bans abortions except in cases of rape, incest, or danger to the woman, and eradicates the use of hospital panels to approve the procedure. In response, the National Right to Life Committee is first convened.

1976 The Hyde Amendment, banning the use of federal funds (like Medicaid) for abortions, is passed, going into effect the following year.

1984 The Mexico City Policy is enacted, barring non-governmental organizations receiving U.S. aid monies from counseling about abortion options.

1989 Following the July *Webster v. Reproductive Health Services* decision—allowing individual states to impose restrictions on abortion—it is clear that for the first time there is no longer a Supreme Court majority prepared to fully affirm *Roe*.

1992 In *Planned Parenthood of Southeastern Pennsylvania v. Casey*, the Supreme Court affirms the principle of *Roe*, but rules that states can further regulate abortion through consent laws and waiting periods, as long as the restrictions do not constitute an "undue burden" for the woman.

1993 Dr. David Gunn becomes the first abortion provider to be assassinated, shot several times outside of his clinic in Pensacola, Florida.

2000 Mifepristone (the medical abortion pill) is approved by the FDA. In *Stenberg v. Carhart*, the Supreme Court narrowly overturns the bans on so-called "partial-birth" abortions in thirty-one states. By a margin of only one vote, the court rules that any ban on a method of abortion must have an exception to protect a woman's life or health.

2006 The FDA finally approves over-the-counter sale of emergency contraception to women and men eighteen and older, after years of stalling from the government and pressure from activists such as the Women's Liberation Birth Control Project.

2007 The Supreme Court, in *Gonzales v. Carhart*, upholds the Partial-Birth Abortion Ban Act of 2003—the first federal legislation to criminalize abortion. By doing so, the court makes one of the safest late-term abortion procedures illegal and overrides decades of precedent that honored medical expertise.

PLANNING A PRO-CHOICE EVENT

January 22 is the anniversary of the *Roe v. Wade* decision and it seems a bit more poignant every year, as restrictions continue to mount and more Supreme Court challenges emerge. One way to fight the gloom is to make the *Roe* anniversary powerful—a day of consciousness-raising and fundraising. I have compiled a list of actions that might help make a difference.

• Read and discuss books like *Sacred Work: Planned Parenthood and Its Clergy Alliances* by Tom Davis (Rutgers University Press, 2005), which describes the historic (and surprisingly radical) connection between the clergy and the abortion rights movement; *Undivided Rights: Women of Color Organize for Reproductive Justice* by Jael Silliman, Marlene Gerber Fried, Loretta Ross, and Elena Gutiérrez (South End Press, 2004), an excellent volume on the efforts of minority pro-choice advocates; or read individual women's abortion stories in Krista Jacobs's *Our Choices, Our Lives: Unapologetic Writings on Abortion* (iUniverse, 2004), Angela Bonavoglia's *The Choices We Made: Twenty-five Women Speak Out About Abortion* (Seal Press, 2001), and the zine *Our Truths/Nuestras Verdades*.

• Host a viewing of Nancy Savoca and Cher's *If These Walls Could Talk*, the *I Had an Abortion* documentary, or Mike Leigh's *Vera Drake* in your own home or at a screening room at a local university or movie theater. Consider making it a fundraiser for initiatives like the Abortion Conversation Project's "Mom, Dad, I'm Pregnant," which encourages dialogue between pregnant girls and their parents.

• Call your local Planned Parenthood or independent abortion clinic and thank them for what they are doing. Write a letter or op-ed to the local paper praising the work of the local clinic and, if you have one, tell your own abortion story.

• If you're theatrical or a college student or just ambitious, stage a production of *Words of Choice,* Cindy Cooper's collection of short plays (made into a film in 2007), which could easily become the new *Vagina Monologues.* While each piece is riveting on its own, taken together the performance makes clear the political impact of restrictions, clinic violence, and regressive laws that hurt women. For more information, go to www.wordsofchoice.org.

These are only a few suggestions for great *Roe* events, and there are several other suitable dates for hosting events. For instance, March 8 is International Women's Day; Young Women's Day of Action typically falls in October; and the National Day of Appreciation for Abortion Providers is March 10.

FURTHER READING

My grandmother was shocked (in a good way) the first time she came across the *Our Bodies, Ourselves* series, the definitive guidebooks to women's health needs, written by the Boston Women's Health Book Collective. It's still the first and the best when it comes to being the expert on your own body.

Our Bodies, Ourselves
34 Plympton St.
Boston, MA 02118
tel: 617-451-3666; fax: 617-451-3664
e-mail: office@bwhbc.org
www.ourbodiesourselves.org

Portland-based writer Judith Arcana, a former Jane Collective member, is the author of *What If Your Mother* (Chicory Blue Press, 2005), an incredible collection of poems that deal with abortion. For another look at the organization, check out *Jane: Abortion and the Underground* (1999), a play by Paula Kamen, the third-wave feminist author of *Feminist Fatale: Voices from the Twentysomething Generation Explore the Future of the Women's Movement* (Donald I. Fine Books, 1996) and *Her Way: Young Women Remake the Sexual Revolution* (Broadway, 1992). Kamen's extensive interviews with Jane members are archived at Northwestern University.

Our Truths/Nuestras Verdades is a biannual, bilingual print and online magazine dedicated to bringing to light the diversity of abortion experiences while creating a safe space for all people, regardless of gender, to speak their truths. It was started in 2005 by Emily Barcklow in response to her own abortion and eventually put out by Exhale (and published by its cofounder Aspen Baker).

e-mail: truths_verdades@4exhale.org
www.ourtruths.org

Several reproductive health programs have their own youth- and pop culture–centric blogs, including NARAL's *Bush v. Choice*, run by Jessica Valenti of the feminist blog *Feministing*; Our Bodies Ourselves' blog *Our Bodies Our Blog*; and RH Reality Check's *Reproductive Health Blog*. There are also privately run blogs, such as *Reproductive Rights Blog*, which has a great weekly news roundup.

Bush v. Choice: www.bushvchoice.com
Feministing: www.feministing.com
Our Bodies Our Blog: www.ourbodiesourblog.org
Reproductive Health Blog: www.rhrealitycheck.org/blog
Reproductive Rights Blog: cara.typepad.com

There are other websites that spotlight the personal accounts of women who have had abortions. *I'm Not Sorry* publishes the stories of women who don't regret their decisions. Women who have terminated their pregnancies due to fetal anomalies share their experiences with others at *A Heartbreaking Choice*. The blog *Abortion Clinic Days* includes fascinating stories from two anonymous abortion providers and the women they treat. You can also create your own storytelling portal by making a video of your abortion story story, putting it up on YouTube. One I started can be found at www.youtube.com/SpeakOutAbortion.

www.imnotsorry.net
www.aheartbreakingchoice.com
abortionclinicdays.blogs.com

Since its founding in 1971 (as an insert in *New York* magazine), *Ms.* magazine has been a great source for coverage and commentary supporting reproductive rights. In the first stand-alone issue of *Ms.*, in fact, prominent women including playwright Lillian Hellman and tennis star Billie Jean King signed a statement admitting to illegal abortions in the hope of repealing restrictive laws. Nearly thirty-five years later (in 2006), *Ms.* reprised the petition and garnered 5,000 signatures from readers, many of whom had legal abortions but wanted to draw attention to how fundamental this right is for women.

Ms. Magazine
433 S. Beverly Dr.
Beverly Hills, CA 90212
tel: 310-556-2515; fax: 310-556-2514
e-mail: info@msmagazine.com
www.msmagazine.com

Ann Fessler's incredible book, *The Girls Who Went Away: The Hidden History of Women Who Surrendered Children for Adoption in the Decades Before Roe v. Wade* (Penguin, 2006), explores the experiences of these women who, unable to have an abortion or become single mothers due to legal restrictions and social stigma, relinquished their newborn babies. Rickie Solinger's *Wake Up Little Susie: Single Pregnancy and Race before Roe v. Wade* (Routledge, 2000) is also an excellent pre-1973 reproductive history framed in the context of race.

For other historical analyses and groundbreaking coverage of all issues surrounding reproductive freedom, see *On The Issues* magazine. A print publication from 1982 to 1999, its issues are archived at www.ontheissuesmagazine.com, where new online content is also provided.

ORGANIZATIONS

The SisterSong Women of Color Reproductive Health Collective is a network of local, regional and national grassroots agencies, "formed in 1997 to educate women of color and policymakers on reproductive and sexual health and rights, and to work toward the access of health services, information, and resources that are culturally and linguistically appropriate."

SisterSong Women of Color Reproductive Health Collective
1237 Ralph David Abernathy Blvd. SW
Atlanta, GA 30310
tel: 404-756-2680; fax: 404-756-2684
e-mail: info@sistersong.net
www.sistersong.net

More recently, activists have researched the impact adoption has had not just on adopted children or the people who raise them, but on the birth mothers who were sometimes coerced to give up their kids. There are several groups that have rallied around the rights of birth/natural mothers. Some, like Concerned United Birthparents, First Mothers Reunited, and the Sunflower Birthmom Support Group, provide counseling for birth mothers, while others, like the American Adoption Congress, focus on changing public policy and enacting legislation related to adoption practices. Many of the older organizations that used to serve as adoption agencies now have support groups, and contacting the agency that handled the adoption in question is often a good place to start if you are a birth mother.

Concerned United Birthparents
PO Box 503475
San Diego, CA 92150

tel: 800-822-2777; fax: 858-712-3317
e-mail: info@CUBirthparents.org
www.cubirthparents.org

First Mothers Reunited
e-mail: membership@firstmothers.net
www.firstmothers.net

Sunflower Birthmom Support Group
e-mail: NanaWendt@aol.com
www.bmom.net

American Adoption Congress
e-mail: choard@comcast.net
www.americanadoptioncongress.org

The scope of the Feminist Majority Foundation, formed in 1987, includes international reproductive rights, emphasizing that the right to choose falls under the broader framework of the global human rights movement.

Feminist Majority Foundation
1600 Wilson Blvd., Suite 801
Arlington, VA 22209
tel: 703-522-2214; fax: 703-522-2219
and
433 S. Beverly Dr.
Beverly Hills, CA 90212
tel: 310-556-2500; fax: 310-556-2509
www.feminist.org

Choice USA and Vox are very useful resources if you are interested in starting up a pro-choice group on your campus. Choice USA helps train young leaders, while Vox is the student arm of Planned Parenthood.

Choice USA
1317 F St. NW, Suite 501
Washington, DC 20004
tel: 888-784-4494; fax: 202-965-7701
info@choiceusa.org
www.choiceusa.org

Vox
e-mail: vox@ppfa.org
www.plannedparenthood.com/vox

The group Men and Abortion has basic, unbiased information about abortion presented specifically for men, as well as tips on things like coping with a pregnancy decision and finding a counselor.

Men and Abortion
c/o Professor Arthur Shostak, PhD
Drexel University, Department of Culture and Communications
Philadelphia, PA 19104
www.menandabortion.com

The rights of sexual minorities are integrally related to the rights of women. Fight for gay rights any way you can, but start with the Gay, Lesbian & Straight Education Network. GLSEN "strives to assure that each member of every school community is valued and respected regardless of sexual orientation or gender identity/expression."

GLSEN
90 Broad St., 2nd Floor
New York, NY 10004
tel: 212-727-0135; fax: 212-727-0254
e-mail: glsen@glsen.org
www.glsen.org

And, in their own words, the Human Rights Campaign "represents a grassroots force of more than 700,000 members and supporters nationwide. As the largest national gay, lesbian, bisexual, and transgender civil rights organization, HRC envisions an America where GLBT people are ensured of their basic equal rights, and can be open, honest, and safe at home, at work, and in the community."

Human Rights Campaign
1640 Rhode Island Ave. NW
Washington, DC 20036
tel: 800-777-4723; fax: 202-347-5323
e-mail: hrc@hrc.org
www.hrc.org

National Advocates for Pregnant Women takes on some of the thorniest issues surrounding reproductive rights, such as the right of drug-addicted women to give birth without fear of being arrested. Feminist Women's Heath Center has loads of resources, articles, and services to offer women and men when an unplanned pregnancy occurs. The same goes for Choice Link Up, a pro-choice directory.

National Advocates for Pregnant Women
39 W. 19th St., Suite 602
New York, NY 10011
tel: 212-255-9252; fax: 212-255-9253
e-mail: info@advocatesforpregnantwomen.org
www.advocatesforpregnantwomen.org

Feminist Women's Health Center
14220 Interurban Ave. S., #140
Seattle, WA 98168
e-mail: info@fwhc.org
www.fwhc.org

Choice Link Up
1718 Connecticut Ave. NW, Suite 700
Washington, DC 20009
tel: 202-319-0055
e-mail: info@choicelinkup.com
www.choicelinkup.com

Find a clinic by calling the National Abortion Federation or Planned Parenthood hotlines.

National Abortion Federation
1660 L St. NW, Suite 450
Washington, DC 20036
tel: 800-772-9100
e-mail: nat@prochoice.org
www.prochoice.org

Planned Parenthood Federation of America
434 W. 33rd St.
New York, NY 10001
tel: 212-541-7800; fax: 212-245-1845
and
1780 Massachusetts Ave. NW
Washington, DC 20036
tel: 202-785-3351; fax: 202-293-4349
www.plannedparenthood.org

Women on Waves, founded by the inspirational Dutch doctor and artist Rebecca Gomperts, attempts to get around bans in Catholic countries by performing abortions in international waters. Her organization is making a film about how to safely administer a non-surgical abortion (i.e., the abortion pill) at home.

Women on Waves Foundation
PO Box 15683
1001 ND Amsterdam
The Netherlands
tel/fax: 31-20-465-0004
e-mail: info@womenonwaves.org
www.womenonwaves.org

Gomperts also founded Women on Web, an online medical abortion help service for women living in countries where access to safe abortion services is restricted. You can have a virtual consultation through www.womenonweb.org.

FUNDING

The barrier to choice is often financial. Organizations such as the New York Abortion Access Fund, which provides financial assistance for low-income women to obtain abortions, and the Haven Coalition, a New York City–based hosteling service for women who travel for late-term procedures, are on the forefront of providing grassroots-led access. Similar groups have cropped up across the country as more and more restrictions are placed on abortion. The National Network of Abortion Funds (NNAF) is the place to go to learn how to start your own or to donate to existing funds.

New York Abortion Access Fund
tel: 212-252-4757
e-mail: nyaaf@nnaf.org
www.nyaaf.org

Haven Coalition
PO Box 658
New York, NY 10101
tel: 917-371-2035
e-mail: havencoalition@gmail.com
www.havencoalition.org

NNAF
42 Seaverns Ave.
Boston, MA 02130
tel: 617-524-6040; fax: 617-524-6042
e-mail: info@nnaf.org
www.nnaf.org

Ninety-five cents of every dollar raised by Women's Reproductive Rights Assistance Project goes to assist low-income women in paying for either emergency contraception or a safe abortion.

Women's Reproductive Rights Assistance Project
2934 1/2 Beverly Glen Circle, #169
Los Angeles, CA 91403
tel: 323-223-7727; fax: 818-501-3938
e-mail: jhor529@aol.com
www.wrrap.org

PREGNANT AND CONFUSED?

Your first stop might be the extremely useful Pregnancy Options Workbook, which prompts questions that will lead you to the decision you can be most comfortable with:

e-mail: contact@pregnancyoptions.info
www.pregnancyoptions.info

There are many people who will help you talk through your choice and the emotions that follow. Charlotte Taft, an AHB therapist from Dallas, Texas, together with Shelley Oram, started Imagine, a women's training, non-judgmental counseling, and retreat center at the Dragonfly Ranch in New Mexico.

Imagine Counseling
PO Box 428
Glorieta, NM 87535
tel: 505-757-2991
e-mail: taftoram@cybermesa.com or info@imaginecounseling.com
www.imaginecounseling.com

AFTER-ABORTION RESOURCES

Emerge is a free Minneapolis-based discussion and support group for women who have had an abortion. Women meet weekly to "share and discuss their individual experiences in a safe, respectful, and supportive environment with others . . . whether their abortion was forty years ago or yesterday." Women create rituals to acknowledge and resolve their abortion experiences.

Emerge/Pro-Choice Resources
250 3rd Ave. N., Suite 625
Minneapolis, MN 55401
tel: 612-825-2000; fax: 612-825-0159
e-mail: pcr@birdsandbees.org
www.prochoiceresources.org

"Healthy Coping after an Abortion" is just one of the many helpful publications put out by the Abortion Conversation Project. This essay can be downloaded at: www.abortionconversation.com/healthycoping.pdf.

Abortion Conversation Project
1625 K St. NW, Suite 1020
Washington, DC 20006
tel: 866-460-1444
e-mail: info@abortionconversation.com
www.abortionconversation.com

Exhale is an after-abortion talk line that takes no moral or political stance. Men are welcome to call.

Exhale
484 Lake Park Ave., #63
Oakland, CA 94610
Toll-free talk line (in the U.S.): 866-439-4253
Toll calls (outside of the U.S.): 510-446-7977
e-mail: info@exhale.org
www.4exhale.org

Backline wants to address the broad range of experiences and emotions surrounding pregnancy, adoption, and abortion. It provides "a forum in which women and their loved ones can engage in discussion that moves beyond political rhetoric." Backline was cofounded by Abortion Conversation Project coordinator Grayson Dempsey in 2004. Call for an open-minded, open-ended conversation about anything surrounding your reproductive life.

Backline
4934 NE 29th Ave.
Portland, OR 97211
Toll-free talk line (in the U.S.): 888-493-0092
Toll calls (outside of the U.S.): 503-287-4344
www.yourbackline.org

MEDIA ABOUT ABORTION

TELEVISION SHOWS

In 1972, the hit television show *Maude* famously became one of the first programs to have a lead character go through an abortion.

The HBO miniseries *If These Walls Could Talk* connects three abortion stories, each from a different decade (and each starring its own mega-celebrity).

"The Last Abortion Clinic," a *Frontline* special on PBS, looks at why there is only one remaining abortion clinic in Mississippi and what this means for abortion rights nationwide. You can watch the entire program at: www.pbs.org/wgbh/pages/frontline/clinic.

The teen television series *Degrassi: The Next Generation* has a great episode ("Accidents Will Happen") involving abortion.

HBO's *Six Feet Under* also featured an abortion story line during its third season.

FILMS

Penny Lane's touching thirty-minute documentary *The Abortion Diaries* features the stories of twelve women who have had abortions as well as excerpts from her own diary. E-mail lennypane@gmail.com for general inquiries or development@yourbackline.org to purchase a DVD. www.theabortiondiaries.com

Silent Choices, a film by Faith Pennick about black women and their relationship to abortion, combines both historical information with present-day issues (such as the lack of Medicaid funding for abortions, sterilization abuse, and the criminalization of drug-addicted pregnant women). www.silentchoices.com

There is an incredible 1996 documentary about the Jane Collective called *Jane: An Abortion Service,* created by Kate Kirtz and Nell Lundy. The film is available through Women Make Movies. www.wmm.com

Jenny Raskin and Liz Mermin created the film *On Hostile Ground* (2001) after the 1998 murder of abortion provider Dr. Barnett Slepian in his home. The film interviews three different health care professionals who talk about their personal fears and concerns as abortion providers. The film is available through Aubin Pictures. www.aubinpictures.com/ohg

Most mainstream feature films don't depict abortion (although 2007 saw a mini-trend of hit films involving unplanned pregnancies, from *Waitress* to *Knocked Up* to *Juno*). In 1996, Alexander Payne took on the abortion debate in his satire *Citizen Ruth* (in which Laura Dern portrays a pregnant woman courted by both pro-life and pro-choice forces; in 2004, Todd Solondz directed *Palindromes;* and *Vera Drake* is the 2004 Mike Leigh film telling the story of an Englishwoman in London who provided abortions for young women in the 1950s.

Sacred Choices and Abortion: 10 New Things to Think About, produced by the Religious Consultation on Population, Reproductive Health & Ethics in 2005, looks at the spiritual and religious aspects of abortion, arguing that many movements, including Unitarian Universalism and Reform Judaism, support women's right to choose. (The book version by Daniel Maguire, *Sacred Choices: The*

Right to Contraception and Abortion in Ten World Religions, explores how these communities support and advocate for reproductive rights.)

Dear Doctor Spencer: Abortion in a Small Town (1998) by Danielle Renfrew and Beth Seltzer is a twenty-six-minute award-winning documentary that explores this famed compassionate abortion doctor's life. Filmmaker Dorothy Fadiman has also dedicated her life to creating films about reproductive freedom. Her trilogy of fillms—*When Abortion Was Illegal: Untold Stories* (1992), *From Danger to Dignity: The Fight for Safe Abortion* (1995), and *The Fragile Promise of Choice: Abortion in the U.S. Today* (1996)—are classics. All of these films can be ordered from Concentric Media. www.concentric.org

STORYTELLING

If you liked this book, you will definitely want to see the documentary *I Had an Abortion* (2005), produced by me and directed by Gillian Aldrich. This is a film with the real experts on abortion telling their own stories, not as politically motivated debate artists, but as women who have experienced it firsthand. To share your story, e-mail: gandj@speakoutfilms.com or jenandamy@soapboxinc.com. You can also order a copy of the film through Women Make Movies. www.wmm.com

THE CLERGY

Clergy people have been some of the first and most staunch abortion rights activists. To continue that tradition, contact the Religious Coalition for Reproductive Choice or Catholics for a Free Choice.

Religious Coalition for Reproductive Choice
1025 Vermont Ave. NW, Suite 1130
Washington, DC 20005
tel: 202-628-7700; fax: 202-628-7716
e-mail: info@rcrc.org
www.rcrc.org

Catholics for a Free Choice
1436 U St. NW, Suite 301
Washington, DC 20009
tel: 202-986-6093; fax: 202-332-7995
e-mail: cfc@catholicsforchoice.org
www.catholicsforchoice.org

FULL FRONTAL OFFENSE: TAKING ABORTION RIGHTS TO THE TEES

by Rebecca Hyman

(This essay originally appeared in Bitch: Feminist Response to Pop Culture, *Issue no. 27, Winter 2005.)*

There's a new front in the battle for abortion rights—the literal front, that is, of a T-shirt designed by writer and feminist activist Jennifer Baumgardner that proclaims, *I had an abortion.* The shirt, initially for sale on Planned Parenthood's national website and now available on *Clamor* magazine's website, has generated controversy among not only the anti-abortion community but also pro-choice feminists.

Inspired in part by the bold irreverence of second-wave feminists, who circulated a petition proclaiming the fact of their own abortions and published it in the first issue of *Ms.*, Baumgardner created the T-shirt in order to remove the stigma that relegates those who have had an abortion to shame and silence. The shirt is one component of a multipart project Baumgardner conceived to draw attention to women's experiences of abortion. Other elements of the project include a film that will debut on the anniversary of *Roe v. Wade* in January, featuring interviews with women who have had abortions; a guidebook to busting through the gridlock on the abortion debate, with a photo essay by Tara Todras-Whitehill, that will be published by

Akashic Books; and the creation and distribution of resource cards that help women locate abortion services and obtain post-abortion counseling.

Only the shirt, however, has become a phenomenon. Because of its public nature, the tee has sparked a national response that neither Baumgardner nor Planned Parenthood anticipated.

"The shirt was always the least significant part of the project," Baumgardner says, explaining that she printed 500 shirts, mailing some to influential feminists and selling the rest at last April's March for Women's Lives in Washington, D.C. Soon afterward, Planned Parenthood offered to carry the shirt on their website to "remind everyone that abortion policy affects real people," according to Gloria Feldt, president of the organization. When the *Drudge Report* posted a photograph of the shirt on its opening page, however, a "media tsunami" soon followed, according to a Planned Parenthood media representative.

The shirt has certainly fulfilled Baumgardner's hope that it would start a conversation about abortion, but the very brevity of its message has had an unanticipated consequence. Although it's no surprise that individuals such as Jim Sedlak, executive director of the American Life League's STOPP International, think the shirt "celebrates an act of violence" and demonstrates that Planned Parenthood "lacks any sense of integrity, tact, and compassion," it's interesting to note that many pro-choice feminists are ambivalent about—or even angered by—the shirt's message. Why, they ask, is the abortion fight taking place on something as public and casual as a T-shirt?

In one respect, creating a T-shirt to proclaim the reality of abortion in the plainest of language is the perfect antidote to the climate of fear that informs the ongoing battle for women's reproductive rights. The Bush administration's attack on public health—including sex education, as well as abortion—is taking place in multiple arenas. Family-planning organizations that receive federal funding are forbidden from presenting information about abortion to their clients. President Bush has refused to provide federal funding for research on new stem-cell lines because the cells are garnered from embryonic tissue. The successful passage in Congress of the Partial-Birth Abortion Ban Act has caused doctors who perform abortions to fear for their medical licenses because the law's wording is so vague. The recent passage of the Unborn Victims of Violence Act, which allows a defendant to be charged with two federal crimes when a fetus is killed or injured during an attack on a pregnant woman, presents an even greater challenge to *Roe v. Wade,* because it creates a precedent in which the fetus is granted the legal status of a person. The House has also passed a bill that allows health care providers who oppose abortion not only to refuse to give their patients information about abortion or perform the procedure but also to deny them emergency contraception; it would also prevent government officials from penalizing health care institutions for refusing to provide information or services to their patients. The Republican Party platform contains a plank calling for an explicit ban on all forms of abortion, even if the health of the mother is endangered.

In the face of such a far-reaching antichoice agenda, the presence of women wearing T-shirts proclaiming their decision to have an abortion would seem a forceful response. As Barbara Ehrenreich recently reminded readers in a *New York Times* editorial, "Abortion is legal—it's just not supposed to be mentioned or acknowledged as an acceptable option." Since *Roe v. Wade,* she wrote, "at least thirty million American women" have had abortions, "a number that amounts to about forty percent of American women." Yet according to a 2003 survey conducted by a pro-choice organization, "only thirty percent of women were unambivalently pro-choice." Ehrenreich logically surmises that many women who refuse to state publicly that they are pro-choice have nevertheless obtained safe, legal abortions. By remaining silent about their experience, or by refusing to call the act of terminating a pregnancy because of fetal birth defects an abortion, these women are tacitly supporting those who seek to outlaw abortion. To be vocal about abortion— not by supporting an abstract "freedom of choice," but instead by naming abortion as a fact of women's experience—is thus to break the dual threat of political and private shaming that keeps women silent.

That both Ehrenreich and Baumgardner have called upon women to speak publicly about their abortions is no coincidence; rather, it represents their desire to honor, and perhaps resuscitate, a tactic integral to the politics of second-wave feminism. Many of the political agendas of second-wave feminists were the by-product of consciousness-raising groups, which encouraged women to speak out—not only to break the silences that foster discrimination but also to build community. This legacy of speech-as-activism is still found in Take Back the Night vigils—in which women name their experiences of physical and sexual abuse—as well as in the explosion of feminist zines and the music of riot grrrls.

Like Ehrenreich, who called for women to "take your thumbs out of your mouths, ladies, and speak up for your rights," Baumgardner sees a direct correlation between the increase in women's speech and the increase in their rights. "When women were most vocal about their experiences of abortion," she said, "*Roe v. Wade* was enacted. Now that women are silent about their experiences of abortion, we are seeing a decline in their reproductive rights." Given this history of feminist politics, it's no surprise that Planned Parenthood, which initially agreed to sell 200 shirts on its website, sold out so quickly that it had to refer potential customers to Baumgardner's site to meet the demand. Ehrenreich wears her shirt to the gym; Ani DiFranco wore hers to an interview with *Inc.*, an apolitical business magazine. When the photograph of DiFranco sporting the shirt and holding her guitar appeared, readers wrote to the editors to protest, sparking an extended dialogue about abortion rights on *Fresh Inc.*, the magazine's blog.

One of the most fascinating things about the shirt is the fact that it says so little and yet is interpreted in such radically different ways. I spoke with many women in the Atlanta area about the shirt, most of whom were pro-choice feminists, and heard it called tacky, cavalier, simplistic, arrogant, cool, shameful, and brave. One twenty-four-year-old woman found the shirt offensive because it returns the abortion debate to the public realm. "The whole purpose of abortion rights," she told me, "is to ensure that a woman can make her own decision about her body, in private, without having to seek permission from anyone else—not even her partner." A woman wearing the T-shirt, she explained, is asking for comments of approval or disapproval from men and women. "My body is mine," she said, "and I shouldn't have to justify or announce my decisions to anyone else."

Another woman told me that, though she's pro-choice herself, she couldn't understand why a woman would announce her abortion unless she was doing so as a matter of pride. "Does she want me to think about the fact that she had an abortion every time I see her?" she wondered out loud. "Because if I saw her wearing the shirt, that is what would stay with me, even if she never wore it again." I asked why she was associating a factual statement with the sentiment of boastfulness. "Because it's on a T-shirt," her friend chimed in. "Like the one I have that says, *No One Knows I'm a Lesbian*." Her statement was greeted by nods of approval from the other women who were listening to our conversation. Because there are so many T-shirts that function as affirmations of identity, people have a hard time seeing the shirt outside of a preexisting context. The logical question to ask, then, is the extent to which the fact of having an abortion is an aspect of a woman's identity. The decision to have an abortion is complex. A woman may respond to having an abortion with relief, guilt, grief, or any number or combination of emotions, each of which will contribute in some way to her identity.

And what about the shirt as a fashion statement? If a woman wears the shirt because she likes it but hasn't had an abortion herself, she could be seen as an ally in struggle, or she could be faulted for appropriating another woman's experience—or, worse, disregarding it altogether. It all depends upon the way others perceive her. An activist from California told me that she wants to see as many women as possible wearing the shirt, regardless of whether they've had an abortion, to "participate in the collective destigmatizing of the procedure." To represent the fact of abortion, as the shirt certainly does, is not equivalent to representing experience. It's only an opening line.

But the question of representation is not limited to the shirt itself. The woman who wears the shirt creates a context for its reception in multiple ways. Her appearance, the location in which she wears it, and the fact of her being alone or in a group all add to the shirt's meaning. A woman wearing the shirt in a progressive city like Madison, Wisconsin, or Olympia, Washington, or in a "hate-free-zone" neighborhood like Atlanta's Little Five Points would probably get a reaction, but she'd be as likely to receive positive as negative comments.

What about the shirt's power to belie the stereotype of the kind of woman who has an abortion? A married suburban mother keeping a distracted eye on the children spilling out of her minivan is just as likely to have had an abortion as a single woman in her early twenties. If it comes as a shock to picture the shirt worn by a middle-aged, middle-class woman, it's a testament to the success of conservative rhetoric in casting women who choose abortion as irresponsible, selfish, or overly careerist.

The negative reaction many feminists have to the shirt reveals a fundamental contradiction in the current state of pro-choice politics—or, more precisely, the extent to which those who are pro-choice feel ashamed, at some level, to support abortion. The fact that so many women read a simple statement as a "celebration" of the procedure speaks volumes about the feelings women have internalized as a consequence of the conservative assault on women's rights. Although most of the women I spoke with were uneasy about their response to the shirt, repeatedly insisting that they were pro-choice even as they told me they would never wear it, some reacted to a photograph of the shirt with anger.

"The only reason anyone would wear such a shirt would be to piss people off," one nineteen-year-old woman snorted. "No one who was serious about supporting abortion rights would wear it." Those who saw the shirt as an aggressive tactic also thought it was perfect ammunition for the antiabortion movement, playing into the propaganda that paints pro-choice women as glorying in the selfish taking of a life. And judging from the comments on conservative blogs like *Outside the Beltway*, this argument has some merit.

Amidst the usual vitriol and sardonic humor (one person wrote that the back of the shirt should say, *Roe v. Wade—Eliminating Future Democrats One Choice at a Time*) is a sense that, by creating a T-shirt so many would see as offensive, the pro-choice movement has intentionally sought to outrage the Christian Right.

In fact, the fear that the shirt could inflame the existing passions of the antichoice movement has led some Planned Parenthood affiliates to condemn it. Here in Georgia, I first learned about the shirt when Denise Noe wrote an editorial in the August 2, 2004 edition of the *Atlanta Journal-Constitution* criticizing the shirt and calling for "famous women who have had babies and given them up for adoption [to] announce this fact." On August 13, the paper's "Woman to Woman" column featured a point/counterpoint discussion of the shirt by a liberal and a conservative female commentator. Because the shirt's reception in Atlanta was anything but positive, I was curious to see if Planned Parenthood of Georgia was selling it. When I spoke with Leola Reis, the organization's vice president of communications, education, and outreach, she told me the chapter had not been consulted about the national organization's decision to sell the shirts. When media attention to the shirt escalated, she reported, the chapter had a lengthy and difficult discussion about the issues it raised.

"Women have enough trouble trying to secure a safe and legal abortion without having to become the unwitting victims of pro-life wrath," she said. Though she understands the intention behind the shirt, she's not sure it will have a positive effect on the actual experience of women trying to attain abortions in such a conservative time. Chapters of Planned Parenthood in Idaho, North Carolina, and South Carolina have criticized the shirt outright, and Planned Parenthood Canada distanced themselves from the controversy by saying, via their website, that they "cannot comment on the approach" taken by Planned Parenthood of America.

It's important to recognize the extent to which the attention of the pro-choice movement has shifted away from the bodies and lives of women who need abortions and toward those who aim to strip women of the right to control their reproductive lives. So it's not surprising that a large part of the movement is plagued by the notion that antichoicers riled up by the sight of women proclaiming their abortions on their chests will want to step up their efforts to deny them this power. Given this fear, it would seem a smart strategy to keep quiet, stay under the radar, and hope that women will vote antichoice legislators out of office. Such a focus, however, ignores the effect pro-choice speech, including the shirt, might have on a woman feeling isolated and ashamed because she had an abortion or is considering it. A public sisterhood of those who have chosen abortion, for a variety of personal reasons, could do a lot to counteract the hateful rhetoric of the antichoice movement.

Baumgardner's T-shirt is a lightning rod for the emotions that surround the abortion issue—especially among feminists—because it forces the current unspoken contradiction of the pro-choice movement into public speech. It's smart to recognize the current political climate, the fact that abortion providers have been targeted and killed and clinics bombed, and that women's health clinics operate under the awareness that their staff might be assaulted or murdered for doing their job. In the face of real violence and real political majorities, it might seem logical to lie low and safeguard the rights of women by creating an environment in which they can exercise their right to terminate a pregnancy without fearing for their lives. At the same time, some of the most powerful slogans from both the feminist and gay rights movements focus on the act of speaking up: "*Your silence will not protect you.*" Keeping quiet might seem like a smart political tactic, but when women muzzle themselves because they are afraid, their silence can masquerade as the appearance of support for the antichoice agenda.

If we don't break the silence about abortion, our right to control our reproductive destiny will never seem as natural as the right to wear our political opinions on a shirt.